HE HEARD
AMERICA SING

Books by
CLAIRE LEE PURDY

HE HEARD AMERICA SING

Co-author of
MY BROTHER WAS MOZART

HE HEARD AMERICA SING

THE STORY OF STEPHEN FOSTER

BY

CLAIRE LEE PURDY

Pictures by

DOROTHEA COOKE

NEW YORK

JULIAN MESSNER, INC.

PUBLISHED BY JULIAN MESSNER, INC.
8 WEST 40TH STREET, NEW YORK

PRINTED IN THE UNITED STATES OF AMERICA
BY MONTAUK BOOKBINDING CORPORATION, NEW YORK

CONTENTS

		PAGE
	Introduction	1
CHAPTER		
I.	Two Birthdays	5
II.	Remembering	14
III.	Negroes Sing and Dance	31
IV.	"A Penny for Your Thoughts"	44
V.	Keelboat Man from the Massassip'	51
VI.	"When I Was a Boy"	64
VII.	Minstrels in Town!	78
VIII.	Uncle Struthers	91
IX.	Going Away to School	107
X.	"Dreaming the Happy Hours Away"	117
XI.	Friends	130
XII.	Good-bye	144
XIII.	La Belle Rivière	154
XIV.	The Bookkeeper of Cassilly's Row	164
XV.	"All Merry, All Happy and Bright"	174
XVI.	"I Dream of Jeanie——"	188
XVII.	The Deep South	200
XVIII.	"By 'n' by Hard Times——"	214
XIX.	"... My Heart Grows Weary..."	224

ILLUSTRATIONS

"Lieve thumped the bread vigorously on the kneading board" . . . . *Facing page*   16

"Lost in a world of dreams and memory, the old man drew word-pictures for Stephen"   56

"Stephen sat straight and still for fear of missing one little bit of this glorious noise . . *Bet.* 84-85

"Mrs. Foster bundled Stephen into the seat beside William, with heavy blankets and a buffalo robe on top of all   110

"In the pleasant little back room with its clutter of books and music sheets, Stephen made himself at home   124

"I wish you all kinds of luck, Steve," she said softly. "We shall miss you — more than you know" . . . . *Bet.* 146-147

"On the doorsteps of the cabins men and boys strummed their banjos in the warm evening air" . . . . *Bet.* 180-181

"Joe had many a word of advice for Stephen" . .   190

"One day Stephen sat sadly watching the dog play with the children on the East Common" . . .   216

TABLE OF SONGS

AUTHOR'S NOTE: For the sake of historical accuracy the spelling and capitalization, punctuation and grammar of the originals in the Foster Song Book have been carefully reproduced.

	PAGE
Hard Times, Come Again No More	38
The Glendy Burk	61
Old Folks at Home	89
The Merry, Merry Month of May	95
The Tioga Waltz	116
Come Where My Love Lies Dreaming	128
Open Thy Lattice, Love	131
Lou'siana Belle	140
Old Uncle Ned	142
Oh! Susanna	159
Nelly Bly	165
Oh! Lemuel	169

Table of Songs

PAGE

Away Down Souf 171

My Old Kentucky Home 182

De Camptown Races 185

Nelly Was a Lady 186

Old Black Joe 191

Sweetly She Sleeps 197

Ring de Banjo 198

Way Down in Ca-I-Ro 203

Oh! Boys, Carry Me 'Long 209

Massa's in de Cold Ground 212

Old Dog Tray 216

Jeanie with the Light Brown Hair 222

Some Folks 225

Gentle Annie 228

Beautiful Dreamer 233

INTRODUCTION

Up to the present, the study of Stephen Collins Foster's life has been primarily for adults.

The facts of the greater part of the composer's career have been well established; his definitive biography has been written; his complete works have been republished in their original form; check lists of his music have been published; chronologies, bibliographies, and other appendices have been compiled. Important contributions to Foster literature have been made by Foster's own relatives, by librarians, by professional writers, by amateurs, and by collectors of Fosteriana.

These authorities wrote for adult readers. Their publications are indispensable to the serious Foster student or collector; they were not written for the instruction or entertainment of children. It seems unlikely that they would hold for long the interest of the young reader. So, heretofore, the child who wished to learn about the *life* of the composer contributing so much to his American heritage was obliged to read books written "over his head."

The *music* of Stephen Foster has been admirably edited for children. Within recent years, a collection of more than forty of Foster's best melodies, arranged by

1

Will Earhart and Edward Bailey Birge especially for young voices, has been published as a non-commercial enterprise by Foster Hall, for presentation to schools. The editors, helped by their years of experience in teaching music and their knowledge of what children enjoy singing, have prepared a song book which has served to keep alive the love for these "old favorites" in the new generation, and to arouse an interest in Foster himself. Dr. Earhart and Dr. Birge have prepared the way for *He Heard America Sing.*

It is fitting that a love for Foster's music should be encouraged early in life. The songs of this composer, in some respects a child, are deeply appreciated by children, even though they may not analyze the charm of his music, or recognize the four cardinal virtues of his art—poetry and melody, simplicity and sincerity. Familiarity with music of this kind is of unquestioned benefit to the young student, whether he continues his musical education, or not. Teachers in public schools state that Stephen Collins Foster is the favorite composer of most children in their classes.

The child who wishes to learn about the life of his favorite composer has the right to read a concise and interesting story, written in language which he can understand. He should see Stephen Foster, not as an individual composer, isolated from the rest of humanity, mechanically writing songs which had no connection with life, but as a genius who expressed the whole spirit of his country in the years preceding the American Civil War.

2

Introduction

He should see a fascinating picture of an artist who was a product of his time and his environment, ever bound up with the intensely colorful and romantic days "before the War." Foster's music was strongly influenced by his country's way of life, and his country's way of life was occasionally influenced by his music. In learning about Stephen Foster's career, the child has the opportunity to become acquainted with the music, the literature, the history, the politics, the sentiment, and the emotions of Foster's own America.

Such a picture of the composer of *Old Folks at Home* and *Jeanie with the Light Brown Hair* was presented in the literature for adults already published. But it was difficult for the twelve-year-old boy or girl to comprehend.

The publication of *He Heard America Sing*, by Claire Lee Purdy of Montrose, California, now makes it possible for children to become acquainted easily with the composer of their best loved songs, the stories behind the songs, their background, and their significance in the American scene.

He Heard America Sing fills a gap in the Foster bibliography. It provides an easy answer to that question frequently asked by young students which has perplexed teachers and parents—"Where can I find the story of Stephen Foster and his songs?"

Mrs. Purdy has written this book for young people twelve years of age and over. She has made use of known facts and traditions in the lives of Stephen Foster and his

3

family; to heighten dramatic interest she has made use of fiction in describing incidents forming the background for her facts; these episodes are interwoven with contemporary American history.

Frontier days in Western Pennsylvania and Ohio, encounters with Indians in pioneer territory, escapes from pirates in the Gulf of Mexico, river outlaws, early trade routes, the settlement of Pittsburgh, the decline of the keel-boat days on the Mississippi, the rise of the steamboat, the coming of the railroad, blackface minstrelsy, the glamorous river and plantation life of the Old South, the gradual transition from agrarian to industrial economics, the tragedy of the Civil War—all these phases of national life give Mrs. Purdy the background for the activities of Foster, his family, and their associates.

The readers of *He Heard America Sing,* whether the children for whom the book was especially written, or the parents and teachers of those children, will find the life of Stephen Foster interpreted in an interesting, sympathetic manner, and they will see the panorama of the development of the United States during the nineteenth century up to the Civil War.

FLETCHER HODGES, JR.

Foster Hall Collection
University of Pittsburgh, Pittsburgh, Pa.
August 6, 1939

4

HE HEARD
AMERICA SING

The thanks of the author and the publisher are due to Elizabeth C. Moore for the editorial revision of this book and the verification of its material.

Julian Messner, Inc.

CHAPTER ONE

TWO BIRTHDAYS

"Land o' livin'! That sounds like a new baby, sho' as my name is 'Livia Pise!" The little brown girl set down the pail of frothy milk she was carrying to the springhouse. She looked over her shoulder toward the White Cottage. No one was about. There were only a gray cat and the noonday sun on the kitchen steps. But from within the house came the unmistakable sound of a very young baby crying.

Olivia stared harder and her mouth fell open, she was so astonished. A comical little figure she made, too, as she stood there, red ribbons in her glossy hair, a starched calico dress well above her knobby knees, and one of her toes wearing a bandage as big as a sausage. Her legs were so long that some folks said she looked like a skinny chicken, all legs and wings. Her eyes were so big at just that moment that she looked more like a little barn owl than anything else. Suddenly her white teeth flashed.

"Law me! Wonder effen it's a boy. Sound mighty like! Girls cry louder, gener'ly."

Olivia might have gone on talking to herself all afternoon, and if she had, the good sweet milk in the forgotten pail would not have been so sweet by sundown. Fortu-

5

nately for the milk, the little girl was startled after a minute or two by a great commotion.

There was a burst of cheering, followed by the thunder of cannon. The earth under Olivia's feet trembled. Crack! Crack! Muskets were being fired. Olivia covered her ears with her hands. When she took her hands away, the firing of cannons and muskets had ceased. Many voices were singing in the wood at the foot of the hill on which the White Cottage stood among its locust trees. The song was *The Star-Spangled Banner*. Hearty voices sang it with a will, for the day was the Fourth of July in the year 1826. The people of Lawrenceville, near Pittsburgh, were celebrating another birthday—their country's. The baby at the White Cottage was only a minute old, but the United States of America had fifty candles on its birthday cake. And—though the Lawrenceville people did not know it, all these years before the invention of the "electric telegraph"—the day was to be remembered for something besides birthdays. For on this same Fourth of July in 1826, two great Americans died within a few hours of each other—John Adams and Thomas Jefferson, both of them signers of the Declaration of Independence and both of them Presidents of the United States.

Olivia suddenly remembered her duty. She must have thought of something else besides. At any rate, she hurried more than was necessary, and some of the milk was spilled before she placed the pail in the cool water of the springhouse. Then she ran like a young deer toward the wood. Clambering over a split-rail fence, she found the

6

pathway under the elms and maples. In a moment she stood at the edge of a cleared space, where the celebrators made merry.

Rough planks had been thrown across sawhorses to make picnic tables. Beyond the tables was a deep pit in the earth, with a whole beef on a stout green pole reaching from side to side of the trench. A fire, which had burned slowly under the meat for twenty-four hours, sent up faint wisps of smoke, and with the smoke rose the tempting odor of barbecue. Olivia ran her pink tongue over lips, and felt so hungry that she forgot why she had come in such a hurry to the barbecue grounds.

There were three bands playing. As nearly as Olivia could make out, the band at the far end of the clearing was playing *Yankee Doodle*. Another, nearer the barbecue pit, played *Columbia, the Gem of the Ocean*. The third, nearest Olivia, was blasting away at *Hail to the Chief*. The result was hardly music; but that was no great matter, for no one seemed to be listening anyway.

There were a great many people, all making a great deal of noise until someone at the head table rapped loudly for quiet. Olivia saw a smiling, rather stout man get up and begin to make a speech. Then she remembered why she had come. The man was William Barclay Foster, and the baby that had just been born was his.

Mr. Foster's speech was long. He had been elected the year before to the Pennsylvania State Legislature, and he had much to tell the friends and neighbors who had voted for him. Olivia found no opportunity to impart

7

her exciting news. When Mr. Foster sat down, others rose to talk and to toast what they called the "new country." Olivia thought to herself that anything fifty years old was not very new. The baby at the White Cottage—*there* was something new, and much more exciting than the dry speeches.

When the talking was over at last, and the company was eating roast beef and home-made bread and pickles and roasted potatoes and pies and cakes, and drinking scalding coffee from tin cups, Olivia found her chance.

"Marse Foster!" she called softly. Though Olivia used the slave word *marse,* she was not a slave. She lived in a "free" State; but she also lived close to the States where black people were bought and sold like horses and cattle.

"Marse Foster!" the little girl repeated.

The big man heard her at last and came to her side quickly. His eyes had guessed her message before she spoke, and he set off with swinging strides toward his home on the hill. Olivia had to run to keep up with him.

The little girl stayed in the cheery kitchen. She tried to make out what the murmur of voices from the rooms at the front of the house meant. After a while she heard Mr. Foster speak out in a bluff, hearty way.

"Well, Eliza," he said, "our baby has been born on a proud day."

Then Mrs. Foster's tired voice asked a question. "Do you think that America will be glad to share its birthday with this little one of ours?" Of course no one answered. A seer was lacking to foretell that the baby in the White

Cottage was to become a great man, a famous composer of whom both America and the rest of the world would be proud.

While Olivia was listening, a snub-nosed, freckled lad of seven, wearing a coarse blue jacket and a frayed straw hat, opened the kitchen door from the hall. He threw himself down into a chair in an angry sort of way. "Shucks!" he said.

Olivia stared in amazement. This was the first time that she had ever seen Tom Hunter out of sorts. Tom was a bound boy in the Foster household, under contract to work merely for his keep until he should be twenty-one years old. In accordance with the custom of those days, he could not leave the Foster family until he was of age. The Fosters were kind, however, and Tom did not mind being "bound out" as the boys and girls with less generous masters did. He usually went whistling or singing about his work.

"What ails you, Tom?" Olivia asked. "You look 'zactly like a thunder cloud 'bout ready to explode like them cannons down yonder in the woods."

"Oh, I'm jest plumb disgusted, that's all."

Olivia grinned. "A bat could see that in daytime. That ain't no answer."

Tom began to talk, as if to himself. "They call *that* a name! Why couldn't they give him a real name? Like— well, like anything! Like Jack, or Jim, or—"

"Just what *is* you talking about, Tom Hunter? Who is giving who what kind of a name?"

9

For answer, Tom jerked a disdainful thumb toward the front part of the house.

"You mean you saw the new baby?" Olivia was beginning to understand what Tom meant.

"Yep."

"And it's a boy?"

"Sure it's a boy!"

"And he already has a name?"

"Ain't that what I been telling you?"

"Sho' nuff! And what name is it?"

Tom was more disgusted than ever as he told her. "Stephen Collins. Stephen Collins Foster! Mrs. Foster named him."

Olivia came to the defence of her mistress. "Well, I reckon if anybody has a right to name a child it's that child's own mother."

"But what do you think of this? They named him after a little boy who belonged to a friend of Mrs. Foster's." At this point Tom lowered his voice dramatically and continued, *"A little boy who died!"*

"Oh! That's sho' nuff bad! Land, but grown-up white folks do the most peculiarest things!"

"So you don't like our choice of a name either, eh, Lieve?" It was Mr. Foster who had walked unnoticed into the kitchen and heard the two children talking.

Olivia was too much surprised to speak. Tom managed to slide out of his chair and disappear through the outside doorway.

"Never mind." The big man laughed. "You may go and take one look at the baby if you are very quiet.

10

Then I want you to go down to the picnic grounds and tell Miss Charlotte and the children to come home."

Olivia tiptoed to the darkened room where the baby lay sleeping in his cradle. She gently pulled aside a downy coverlet and took a hasty look at the tiny red face and the clenched hands. She shook her head doubtfully and backed away, carefully closing the door of the room as she set off about her errand in the wood below the White Cottage.

At the barbecue ground she found Charlotte with the younger children. The Foster children were like stair-steps in height. Charlotte was the eldest and tallest, being sixteen. Serious Ann Eliza was fourteen. Next came good-natured Henry, ten years old. Energetic Etty, whose real name was Henrietta, was seven. The two youngest boys were little more than babies, Dunning being five and Morrison, who was always called Mit, being three.

Charlotte in her gentle way asked about the new brother who was to be called Stephen. Etty gave Olivia a big sandwich of barbecued beef between two thick slices of white bread. Then Charlotte took the two little boys by the hand and led the way through the pasture toward the home on the hill.

Between bites, Olivia, or Lieve as the children called her, confided her fears to Ann Eliza. Charlotte was almost a grown-up young lady, and Lieve was shy with grown-ups.

"I sho' wish you could persuade your mama to name that baby a different name, Miss Eliza."

"Why, Lieve! Don't you like *Stephen* as a name? We

11

can call him Steve when he gets older, and that's a fine name for a boy."

" 'Tain't the name, exactly, Miss Eliza. It's who he's named for."

"He is named for a sweet little boy who died, Lieve."

"That's just the trouble. It's unlucky. Nobody ought never name a living child after a person who's dead."

"Lieve! I thought you were a good church member and went to church every Sunday."

"Oh, I is, Miss Eliza, and I does, but all the same—"

"You mustn't be so superstitious, then, Lieve. That's all nonsense—the bad luck, I mean. Only ignorant people believe in bad-luck signs."

"Just the same it seems mighty like what Deacon Samuel said last Sunday. He said, 'Maybe they ain't nothing to the notion that a rabbit's foot brings good luck, but all the same any black man that leave his rabbit foot home even on a Sunday is jes' flying in the face of Providence.' Miss Eliza, I can't help feeling that that child is going to have some powerful bad luck in his life."

"Nonsense, Lieve. Why, look at Brother William. He isn't really our brother, you know. He was brought to our home when he was a very little boy, and mother gave him the name of our own brother who was dead. You know very well that Brother William has had only the very best of luck ever since. Pa says he is going to be a great engineer. He is already earning good money—and he's only seventeen years old."

12

"Reckon that's so, Miss Eliza," said Lieve, but her worried eyes showed that she could not cast away all doubt.

Ann Eliza talked on earnestly. "Ma says that a person makes his own happiness. Of course, some sad things come to all of us—like sickness and having to go away from home and those we love. But Ma says if we are strong and courageous, we won't let things like that get the better of us."

Lieve sighed. "Maybe. But, Miss Eliza, it wouldn't *cost* nothing to give that baby a different name—to be real sure?"

Ann Eliza smiled. "Don't worry, Lieve. It will be all right."

There was a short silence. Suddenly Lieve spoke. "Miss Eliza?"

"Yes, Lieve?"

"Would you do something to kinda ease my mind?"

"If I can, Lieve. What is it?"

Lieve fumbled with one of the ribbons in her hair, and drew out a short match stick. It was a sulphur match of the sort known in those days as a *brimstone* splint.

"Take me into the baby's room again so I can put one of these brimstones near his crib. It'll act against the bad luck. Please, Miss Eliza!"

And because Ann Eliza was kind-hearted and did not wish to hurt the little servant girl's feelings, she promised to let her place her foolish charm in the baby's room.

13

CHAPTER TWO

REMEMBERING

SIX YEARS AFTER Stephen was born, the Foster family were living in Harmony, Pennsylvania. Spring had come and gone, and June had brought hard green fruit to replace the pink and white blossoms of peach and pear and plum in the orchard at the back of the new home. Locust trees growing in a fence corner served to remind the children of the White Cottage.

The Fosters no longer owned the White Cottage. They had lost it and all the wide acres around it to the Bank of the United States. That was the unpopular National Bank, to which President Jackson dealt a death-blow later that same year of 1832 when the Fosters had to move from their home.

Ann Eliza and her mother had cried a little on the day they left the White Cottage. "It will never be quite the same for us," Ann Eliza said. "I hate to go."

"All of us do," said her mother gently and sorrowfully.

Then with heavy hearts they followed Etty and Henry and Mit, Dunning, and Stephen, Tom and Lieve, through the white gate to the road where Mr. Foster waited with the carriage.

At the foot of the hill was the pleasant little town of

14

Lawrenceville. The children knew that the land on which it was built had once belonged to their father. He had planned and helped to build the village, and had named it in honor of gallant Captain James Lawrence, who had commanded the famous ship *Chesapeake* in the War of 1812. One hundred and twenty-three acres had once belonged to the Fosters, and now they did not own even the beloved home on the hilltop.

Though they often thought of the old home, with its locust trees and the long road winding to the Allegheny River, the children were soon happy again. They had pigs and chickens and a little brown cow. Henry looked after the pigs and helped Tom Hunter with the heavy tasks. Henry was sixteen and the man of the house, for Mr. Foster had to be in Pittsburgh most of the time, attending to his new job as Canal Commissioner of the Blairsville-Pittsburgh Canal. Ann Eliza kept house for her father in town.

Etty looked after the younger boys at Harmony, keeping them out of mischief and seeing to it that they studied their lessons. Lieve, grown very tall, carried frothing pails of milk as of old, and helped Mrs. Foster with the cooking and sewing and cleaning.

Thus it was a contented household which the late afternoon sun looked in on one bright June day. At the dining-room table Etty and Henry were taking turns reading Hume's *History* aloud to Dunning and Mit. The older children always helped the younger during the study hour. In the square kitchen with its scrubbed pine

15

floor Lieve was thumping and pushing a yeasty lump of dough, the while she sang:

"Old Mr. Frog, he went a-co'tin',
     Uh-huh, uh-huh!
Old Mr. Frog, he went a-co'tin',
     Uh-huh, uh-huh!
Went right down to see Miss Mouse;
Said, 'Miss Mouse, let me in yo' house.'
     Uh-huh!"

With each "uh-huh" Lieve thumped the bread vigorously on the kneading board, to the delight of Stephen, who watched and listened.

"Went right down to see Miss Mouse,
     Uh-huh, uh-huh!
Went right down to see Miss Mouse,
     Uh-huh, uh-huh!
Took Miss Mouse upon his knee,
Said, 'Miss Mouse, will you marry me?'
     Uh-huh!"

Suddenly Lieve turned to Stephen and sang out, "Where shall the wedding supper be?"

And Stephen, knowing it was his turn, replied gleefully, "Down by the branch, in the hollow tree."

"What shall the wedding supper be?" sang Lieve.

"A little green worm and a bumblebee," Stephen replied.

16

Remembering

Stephen's mother, who had been writing letters in her room, paused to listen to the pleasant uproar. Presently she heard Stephen beating on his toy drum, and caught a glimpse of him as he marched past her door. She smiled, recalling a letter which she had written to Brother William the month before, describing Stephen at his favorite make-believe.

"Stevan,"* she had written, "has a drum and marches about after the old way, with a feather in his hat and a girdle about his waist, whistling old lang syne. . . . There still remains something perfectly original about him."

The letter finished, Mrs. Foster took her diary from the bureau drawer. She had written in the same thick padded book since her girlhood, and as she turned its pages all sorts of memories came rushing back to her. Memories of her girlhood friends in Delaware and Maryland. Memories of the early days of her homemaking in the pioneer town of Pittsburgh. Memories of the husband and the children she loved.

Mrs. Foster looked like an old-fashioned portrait miniature, with her ivory-pale face framed by smooth brown hair. As she rocked gently in the maple-wood rocker her dark eyes had a far-away look, dreamy and serene. The children were growing up, she was thinking. William was already a full-fledged engineer, working on canal and river transportation projects. His work would provide for the people of America easier and

* The spelling is that of the original.

better ways to the rich farm lands of Kentucky and Ohio
and the western country beyond the Mississippi River.
She was glad to think how useful and successful he was;
yet it saddened her that his surveying kept him from
home most of the time.

She thought of Charlotte, the beautiful eldest daughter
whose death three years before remained a fresh wound
in her heart. She closed her eyes and saw Charlotte as
she remembered her best, sitting at the piano, that wonderful piano which had come all the way from Europe
to New York, and then by canal-boat and by freight
wagon across the Allegheny Mountains to Pittsburgh.
Generous Brother William had given the instrument to
his sister, a pianist of uncommon ability. Local music
teachers, Mr. Peters and others, had predicted a brilliant
future for the young musician.

Mrs. Foster sighed, remembering that from the first
there had been some deep, unaccountable melancholy in
Charlotte. Her songs had been strange and wistful. Like
the sighing of a gentle wind in the poplars she had gone,
leaving behind her memories of haunting beauty and
gentle ways.

The mother's thoughts came back from the past to
Stephen, her youngest child. He was not unlike his sister
Charlotte, she thought. As a little boy of two he had
often begged for Charlotte's guitar. He would sit on the
floor, plucking the strings of his "ittly pizani," his little
piano. Could it have been accident, she wondered, that
now and again he would pick out the ghost of a tune—a

18

pattern of notes that no one had heard before? Perhaps; but it might be more than accident!

At that point in her reveries she was interrupted by the children—Henry, Etty, Mit, Dunning, and Stephen. Seeing the diary, they demanded a story.

"Tell us about things that happened when you were a girl," suggested Etty, sitting primly on a footstool and drawing her feet daintily under her wide petticoats.

The dark, graceful woman who was their mother laughed down at her brood. Henry sprawled on the floor at her feet and grinned up at her. Dunning and Mit leaned against her knees. Stephen crawled into her lap. Etty moved her stool closer so that she could rest her cheek on her mother's hand.

How different they were, one from another, their mother thought. Henry was like his father, good-natured, cheerful, interested in everything. Etty had roguish eyes and a stern mouth; she could make them all laugh when she was in the mood, and she could also scold. Dunning was romantic, fond of reading books like *Ivanhoe* by Sir Walter Scott. Dunning had big dreams of riding off to adventure some day. Mit was thoughtful, saying very little, hearing and understanding much that others passed over without noticing.

And Stephen—Stevie had the dark eyes of his mother, eyes inherited from an Italian lady of long ago. Stevie dreamed and sang all day long, and only smiled sweetly when Etty took him to task for not knowing his spelling lesson. Even Etty could not remain angry with him long.

19

What was Stevie like? His mother shook her head. She did not know exactly.

The clamoring of her children brought Mrs. Foster's thoughts back to the diary.

"My stories aren't so exciting as your father's," she teased. "No Indian fights or capture by pirates or wild river men. Mostly homey things."

"I like homey things best," said Stephen in such a serious way that all of them laughed.

"Well, then," began Mrs. Foster, with a hug for Stephen, "when I was a girl, I lived in the eastern part of our country, first in Delaware, later in Maryland."

Mrs. Foster had the gift of poets. She could make the everyday happenings and scenes of life interesting in the telling.

When she told her children about Baltimore's tobacco-export business, they saw in their mind's eye the plantation houses built long before the Revolution of 1776 and the fields where tobacco grew in long green rows. They heard the merry laughter of the plantation Negroes rolling the huge hogsheads of tobacco down to rickety private landings on Chesapeake Bay. They saw the wharves of Baltimore piled high with these hogsheads, waiting to be loaded into the square-rigged ships from England.

Mrs. Foster described the fox-hunts in the fall of the year, hunts conducted in the aristocratic manner of "Merrie England." Her children were made to see the pink-coated squires on thoroughbred horses following the hounds through frost-tinted coppice and across brown fields of stubble.

As she told her tales, Mrs. Foster's eyes glowed with the visions of those early scenes of her happy youth. She told about coachmen cracking long whips over the backs of lead and wheel horses drawing carriages to routs and weddings. She recalled candle-lit ballrooms in stately mansions where laughing-eyed maids and their dashing beaux danced the figures of the reel. She described the scraping of the fiddles played all through the night and the breakfast at dawn.

"That was in Maryland, where life went on much as it had in the days of John Calvert, Lord Baltimore, except that the Indians had long since been pushed to the West and were as rare as they are in Pittsburgh today," explained Mrs. Foster. "Later, my family, the Tomlinsons, moved to Delaware. There I remember best the great tall-masted ships that used to sail into port to load the goods hauled from the West in big freight wagons.

"Rough Irish sailors brought those ships into port with a song, but I was not often allowed to listen. It was not considered ladylike for a little girl to hear the singing of men who spent their lives following the boisterous ways of the sea."

"Sing one of those songs," commanded Stephen unexpectedly.

"I declare, Stevie! How you come to life when a song is mentioned!"

21

"I like it when you sing," said Stephen with a coaxing smile.

"Sure, Ma. Don't beat about the bush, now. I'll bet you know a sailor's chanty or two." Henry was in the mood for teasing his mother, who was old-fashioned and easily flustered over anything she considered even slightly unladylike.

"Please sing just one!" insisted Stephen.

Mrs. Foster was blushing like a schoolgirl. "Now, boys, please. I—I'm afraid I have forgotten."

"You mean you *wish* you had." Mit joined in the fun. "Didn't I hear you humming this one to yourself the other day?" Mit roared out in the best sea-faring manner:

> "Haul the bow-line, the good ship's a-rollin',
>   Haul the bow-line, the bow-line haul!
> Heave the bow-line, the fore-and-main-top bow-line,
>   Haul the bow-line, the bow-line haul!"

Henry and Dunning added their voices to the song, paying no attention to their mother's "I didn't! You know I didn't, Mit! Oh, dear, what it is to be the mother of boys!"

To Stephen's delight the song went on:

> "Heave the bow-line, the skipper he's a-growlin',
>   Haul the bow-line, the bow-line haul!"

Etty took it upon herself to rebuke the boys, saying, "It's really *too* bad to carry a joke *too* far," but Mrs.

22

Foster seemed to like the joke in spite of her protests.

"Well, Stevie," said his mother, "you have had your song, after all—and sung very like a wild Irishman, too, Mit."

Etty changed the subject. "Did you ever go traveling?" she asked. "All by yourself, I mean? I think that would be a thrilling thing to do—so improving. Charlotte used to go to Kentucky, and Ann Eliza, too. It seems to me that I am old enough to go somewhere to visit. Pa says I have ever so much common sense, and of course you need common sense in traveling and visiting. It seems to me—"

"Wow!" yelled Henry. "When the young lady gets wound up, there's no stopping her!"

The rest giggled, and Etty smiled in spite of herself. "Well," she laughed, "did you? Go traveling, I mean?"

"Yes, indeed I did." Mrs. Foster patted her daughter's cheek fondly. "And don't you let these young rascals embarrass you, Etty." Mrs. Foster had a way of letting her children know that she loved them all equally, and had no favorites.

"There was nothing I liked better than visiting my aunt and uncle in Philadelphia—the Oliver Evans family, you know."

"Uncle Oliver Evans was the great inventor, wasn't he?" Henry was instantly all ears, for machines and their inventors fascinated him.

"Yes," said his mother. "He was the friend of John Fitch, who invented the steamboat, and he himself built

23

a steam-driven scow that ran on the Delaware River in 1804, three years before Mr. Fulton's *Clermont* was launched on the Hudson River.

"I was a visitor in the Evans home when Uncle Oliver completed his famous 'steam carriage.' It wasn't a real carriage at all. In fact, it had been designed as a dredge to clear snags and sand from the river bottom, but Uncle Oliver put wheels on it and ran it down Race Street to prove his contention that steam would move vehicles on land as well as on water. He had long declared that some day someone would construct carriages to transport people and freight on land. Of course, almost everyone laughed at him. They said he was as crazy as that lunatic, John Fitch, who was always going around trying to get money to build steamboats.

"But they didn't laugh so hard when they saw him walking beside his dredge on wheels as it moved out of his yard and into Race Street. Some of his neighbors joked about it, saying Uncle Oliver should call the contraption The Frog, since it could live both in and out of water. Uncle Oliver didn't care how much fun they made. He knew he was right!"

"And I guess those neighbors know it, too, now—especially since *Tom Thumb's* trip two years ago," observed Henry.

"Tom Thumb?" Stephen spoke in a puzzled way. "Do you mean the little boy that was only as big as his mother's thumb and fell into the pudding and—"

"No, dear." His mother smiled and shook her head

24

to warn the others not to laugh. "Henry means the little steam-engine built by Peter Cooper two years ago at Baltimore. A relative of ours was present at the trial run and wrote us all about it. You see, Mr. Cooper built an engine that could run on rails, to carry passengers and freight just as Uncle Oliver said would be done some day. The engine was so small that Mr. Cooper named it *Tom Thumb*. Small as it was, though, the engine made a very successful trip of thirteen miles to Ellicott City and return."

"And last year," said Henry, eager to show his knowledge of the world's progress, "the *De Witt Clinton* engine pulled a string of stagecoach cars from Albany to Schenectady."

"Even if all the passengers did get their clothes on fire," put in Etty. "Teacher told us at school how the sparks from the pine wood flew from the stack and the passengers had to raise their umbrellas to protect themselves. Then the umbrellas caught fire, and the engine had to stop every few miles so that the passengers could tramp and beat the sparks out."

"And when they finally got to Schenectady," Mit added, "all the buggy horses ran away with the people who had come to welcome the train." He laughed heartily at the picture of the little train arriving with its passengers frantically beating out sparks in their clothing and the frightened horses rearing and running away from the strange monster which was the engine.

"What I think is the funniest thing, though, is that

25

race. You know, when *Tom Thumb* raced with the horse," said Dunning.

"Which of them won?" asked Stephen.

"The horse, of course," laughed Dunning.

"All the same," said their mother, "horse or no horse, we have several very practical railways in America to-day—though some do use horses instead of steam-engines to pull their cars," she added with a smile for Dunning.

"Brother William says that in days to come there will be a steam railroad across the Alleghenies to Pittsburgh," Mit observed.

"Gee!" The thought seemed to stagger Henry. "That would be a task for giants—laying a track across the mountains. I wonder—"

But that track across the mountains was indeed to be laid some twenty-two years later—in 1854—and Brother William was to be one of the Chief Engineers of the famous Pennsylvania Railroad.

Mrs. Foster continued her story of the Evans family, and Philadelphia. "In those days," she reminded her children, "Philadelphia was the capital of our country. Uncle Oliver, who I thought was the jolliest man in the world, used to take me with him when he had business in interesting parts of the town. He pointed out all the sights to me, sometimes pretending that he was a hired guide and calling out the names of places in an important sort of way that made people turn and stare at us or laugh at his foolishness.

"On one of our expeditions we went up the Ridge to

the hill where Benjamin Franklin first caught the lightning with a kite. Another time we visited Norriton, which had been the home of David Rittenhouse, the watchmaker who built a telescope and made himself and America famous because of it.

"It was in the home of this uncle and aunt that I first met your father. He used to bring flowers when he called. I would peer from behind the parlor curtains to watch him coming up the walk to the front door—young and dashing, with an air of adventure about him.

"He worked for the firm of Anthony Beelen and Ebenezer Denny of Pittsburgh, merchants who traded with importers as far away as New Orleans, which belonged to Spain in those days. Twice a year this young Mr. Foster was put in charge of several flatboats loaded with flour and furs and other articles produced near Pittsburgh. With a rough crew of river men he floated down the Ohio River to the Mississippi, and on down that waterway of treacherous snags and sandbars and murderous outlaws and Indians until he reached New Orleans.

"At New Orleans he would sell his cargoes and set sail for Philadelphia, where he bought European goods for the store across the mountains. His talk about adventures in the wild western country used to frighten me, but it attracted me, too. To a girl whose longest trip had been by stagecoach between Wilmington and Philadelphia, he seemed a veritable world traveler.

"We were married in Chambersburg, where I had

27

relatives. That was in the year 1807. The month was November, and on a crisp autumn morning we set out on horseback for my new home over the Allegheny Mountains."

Mrs. Foster opened her diary and read the old-fashioned, stilted phrases of her narrative:

"The journey was slow and monotonous, and it was not until the fourteenth day that I hailed with delight the dingy town of Pittsburgh, my future home, where every joy and every sorrow of my heart since that bright period have been associated with the joys and sorrows of its people. It was evening when, weary and faint with travel, I was conducted, or, rather, borne, into the hospitable mansion of my husband's partner, the benevolent Major Denny, a dwelling in the centre of the town, where I was received and treated with the most extreme kindness. After resting and changing my apparel I was shown into an apartment below stairs where blazed in all its brilliancy a coal fire, casting its light upon the face . . . of little Nancy Denny, at that time five years old. The well-cleaned grating of the chimney-place, the light that blazed brightly from the fire, the vermillion hearth, the plain, rich furniture, the polished stand with lighted candles in candlesticks resembling burnished gold, made an evening scene that fell gratefully on my pleased sight. Upon a sofa lay the tall and military figure of the Major, a gentleman of the old school, easy and dignified in his bearing, a soldier who had served his country well under Washington at Yorktown, and Harmar, St. Clair and Wayne in the subsequent Indian campaigns."

"I liked Pittsburgh at once," said Mrs. Foster, laying the diary aside. "Though it was already a thriving city, with considerable shipping and manufacturing, it had retained much of the old spirit of pioneer days when it was only a few log cabins clustered around a fort. People still were simple in their living.

"I remember how this simplicity and sincerity impressed me. It showed itself, this pioneer spirit, on a day when all the town was saddened by the death of a young girl who died on the eve of her wedding day." Mrs. Foster read once more from her diary:

"The borough could only boast of two double carriages ready for use. . . . I think there were other carriages, but like old pianos, they were out of use. . . . Be that as it may, the company in attendance all walked, except the mourners. The procession moved without pomp; not even a pall covered the coffin. The pride of these people did not lean to vain glory. . . ."

Could it have been this story that Stephen, the six-year-old boy sitting quietly in his mother's lap, remembered in later years when he was a famous musician and composer? At any rate, he wrote the words and music of *The Village Maiden,* a sad little song with a story similar to that told in his mother's diary.

The children and Mrs. Foster were recalled to their surroundings by a loud sniff. The sniff emanated from Lieve, who had come to say that dinner was ready and had remained in the doorway to hear the story of the bride.

"Why, Lieve!" exclaimed Mrs. Foster in concern. "What ever is the trouble?"

29

The children stared round-eyed at the servant girl.

"Law me!" Lieve began to wipe her eyes with her apron. "That story done gone and got me all melancholish, Mrs. Foster. And I come in here all cheerful to say the bread about baked and the chicken *smell* good enough to eat."

"Thank goodness for that," said Mrs. Foster in relief. "I was half afraid you'd maybe burned the dinner to a crisp. I declare, Lieve, you do beat the Dutch sometimes."

"Yes'm. Reckon I do, Mrs. Foster," said Lieve, going back to her kitchen without knowing in the least what one had to do to beat the Dutch.

"And that goes for us, too," laughed Mrs. Foster, sliding Stephen from her lap. "Time to wash up for dinner, you funny goslings. We have done quite enough remembering for one day, anyway."

CHAPTER THREE

NEGROES SING AND DANCE

WHEN THE EARLY autumn frost had crisped the leaves of the buttonwoods and maples and left the cottonwoods along the rivers bare, the Fosters moved to Allegheny City, just north of the main settlement of Pittsburgh. Here they lived for almost three years, first in a frame house very near "The Point" (where the Allegheny River and the Monongahela River join to form the great Ohio) and later in a house just outside of town.

During these years, Brother William was working in Kentucky. His frequent letters with money for the family in Allegheny showed how much he loved his foster parents and brothers and sisters. Ann Eliza married and had her own home in Meadville. Her husband was Edward Buchanan, whose brother James was later to become President of the United States. Henry went into Pittsburgh to learn the trade of tanning leather from a Mr. Singer. Etty and the three youngest boys were at home. Etty went to Miss Parry's school and the boys attended the Allegheny Academy. Tom and Lieve were still with the family, though Tom was already dreaming

31

of the Far West to which he ran away in his sixteenth year in search of fortune and adventure.

Stephen enjoyed the cool days of that first autumn in Allegheny City. He liked walking to school in the morning sunshine. The roads were filled with brown autumn leaves, and he liked their pleasant rustle as he shuffled through them. Morning sounds from the rivers made his heart pound with excitement. Stephen had been down to the levees along the Ohio River many times, and the sound of the whistles and bells of the river boats reminded him of the busy yet care-free life always to be found there.

He knew by name nearly all the "Buckeye" river boats, as the steamboats on the Ohio River were called. These gayly painted craft with their flat bottoms and paddle wheels at the stern brought cargoes from down river and unloaded them at Pittsburgh. Some of the freight had been brought up the long Mississippi River from New Madrid and Natchez and even from far-off New Orleans.

There were often passengers from the "Deep South," most of them planters from Louisiana, with broad-brimmed hats and long moustaches. These men never pronounced their r's. They said, "Yes, Suh!" and "We would be pleased to entuhtain you-all in ouah home, whenevah you come down rivah." They were gallant gentlemen, who were quick to help the languid, graceful Southern ladies on and off the boats—ladies on whose account, Stephen well knew, many a duel had been fought in the quaint city of the levees. There were always slave servants with the people from the South. Stephen would stare at them and wonder how it felt to be sold at auction like a hogshead of tobacco.

The boats brought with them Negro deck hands and roustabouts with a flavor of the South. Stephen had heard these Negroes singing at their work, nostalgic songs mostly about the plantations where cane grew in the fields and cotton had to be picked. They sang of the corn-top blossom and the cane in the brake, of simple pleasures and of work. Songs of the fiddle. Songs of the hoe.

When the Negroes were not unloading the cotton, molasses, sugar, and tobacco from the ports along the Mississippi and Ohio rivers, they played banjos and danced the juba. The juba was a grotesque dance during which the performer slapped his knees and slapped his hips, shouting, "Juba here and juba there!" It was a lively African rhythm. Stephen stored it in his mind.

Once when he heard a very old Negro singing, he listened until he learned the words of the song. They went:

> "Come, butter, come,
> De King and de Queen
> Is er-standin' at de gate,
> Er-waitin' for some butter
> An' a cake.
> Oh, come, butter, come."

The man sang with his wrinkled eyelids closed, as if he were picturing to himself the old plantation and the

33

cabin where Mammy ironed clothes while the picka-
ninnies took turns at dashing the butter paddle up and
down in the churn while they sang their nonsense song.

Winter's cold winds and snow made Stephen glad to
spend most of his days beside the glowing kitchen range
or in a cozy window-seat. No matter what the weather,
though, when Sunday morning came, Stephen went to
church. Sometimes he went with his mother and Etty
and his brothers. Sometimes he was allowed to go with
Lieve to her church of shouting colored folk. A wave of
religious hysteria was sweeping over America, and the
emotional Negro was quick to imitate the shouting and
rolling and other grotesqueries seen at white folks' camp
meetings.

Stephen liked to go to Lieve's church because the
Negroes sang. The congregation of his mother's con-
servative church sang, too, but not such songs as were
heard in the gray frame building near the Allegheny
River. When the Negroes sang, it was as if they were
lifted out of the hard, everyday struggle of living, forgetting pain and sorrow for the moment. When they
sang, there was magic in the air, and something in seven-
year-old Stephen hungered for this strange magic of
song.

So it was that one cold morning in the year 1832 found
Lieve and Stephen stepping along churchward on the
first light snow of winter. Stephen was bundled up
warmly, with a woolen muffler about his neck and a
bright cap to cover his ears.

34

"What do you suppose they will sing today, Lieve?" Stephen looked up into the servant's smiling eyes.

"Shame on you, Stevie Foster. I believe you go to church just to hear the singing!" Lieve was teasing, but she pretended to be serious.

"I like the preaching, too—honest I do, Lieve," Stephen declared. "Only, when the preacher tells me to be good, I just agree with him and don't feel a bit like being different from what I am. But when the people sing, about Jordan and Egypt Land and Old Pharaoh, I get to feeling ashamed that folks can be so mean to one another, and I want to be good and help others be good, too."

"You give me the queerest feeling, sometimes, Master Stevie. You talk like a preacher yourself once in a while." Lieve's eyes showed the genuine concern she felt. Lieve was still superstitious, in spite of Ann Eliza's efforts, and she had the queer notion that very bright children were marked for early death.

"You like the singing, don't you, Lieve?"

" 'Course I do."

"Where do your people get their songs, Lieve? The hymn-books don't have any of the songs I hear at your church."

"Natur'ly they don't." Lieve spoke with pride. " 'Cause the songs we sing aren't writ down. They come right out of our hearts. Sometimes we make them up as we go along. Then we remember the best ones, and sing them over and over."

"Some day," said Stephen seriously, "I am going to write songs like that. I have songs right in my heart, too, Lieve."

There was a group of colored folk gathered on the steps of the church when Lieve and Stephen arrived. When they saw Stephen, they crowded round him with affectionate greetings.

Most of them were shabbily dressed, for hard times had struck the humble people in the great land of the United States. The men were dressed in the cast-off trousers and coats of white employers. The women were mostly in home-made woolen dresses, with shawls and bonnets on their heads, and each one wore some pin or ribbon of which she was proud. All carried Bibles or Testaments, even though some could not read one word in the book in their hands.

"How is your mama's toothache?" one of them asked Stephen in a friendly way. And another—"My, oh my! I heah tell Miss Ann Eliza is sho' nuff engaged! I 'spec' you-all will be right lonesome for her, once she's done gone and got herself married." And then it was time to go inside and sit on the hard wooden benches in front of the high pulpit, where the minister in his somber black clothes was already opening the big Bible.

First there was a prayer from one of the deacons of the church. He was a great while saying very little, but finally he was done. Then the minister read from the Psalms, something about "make a joyful noise," and all at once the people were singing. Stephen sat on the edge of his seat and seemed to drink in the rich melody.

The refrain of their song was a repetition of the same words, over and over, but each time the people sang it, they made it seem different. The voices of the women began:

> "In that great gittin'-up mornin'—
> Fare you well, fare you well!"

And the deep, rich voices of the men came:

> "In that great gittin'-up mornin',
> Fare you well!"

One of the congregation suddenly shouted, "Wanta go to heaben!"

Others took up the cry. Gradually the words grew into a song, a sad spiritual. Reverently the Negroes sang:

> "Lis'en to de lam's—all a-cryin',
> Lis'en to de lam's—all a-cryin',
> Lis'en to de lam's—all a-cryin',
> I wanta go to heaben when I die."

After that they sang a song of their own, one they made up as they went along. Most of the people did not sing words to this one, but just hummed the melody as it caught them up. It was a sad melody. Many of the people were hungry. Some had not enough to wear or enough coal at home to keep them warm. Their song was about these things. One old man who sat near Stephen did not sing, but mumbled a few words, low and in rhythm with the other voices.

"Hard times," he said, as if he might be praying, "come again no more!"

Stephen, sitting straight and still beside Lieve, never forgot that melody and the old man praying. He stored the memory in his mind. Years later, when he had become a man, he still remembered a snatch of that Negro song. It must not be lost forever, he thought; so he added more to it out of his own heart and wrote words for it. He called it by the words of the old man's prayer. This is the great and beautiful song in which Stephen Foster preserved his boyhood memory of Lieve's sad people singing:

HARD TIMES, COME AGAIN NO MORE

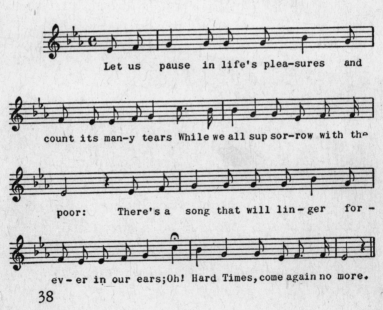

Let us pause in life's plea-sures and count its man-y tears While we all sup sor-row with the poor: There's a song that will lin-ger for- ev-er in our ears; Oh! Hard Times, come again no more.

38

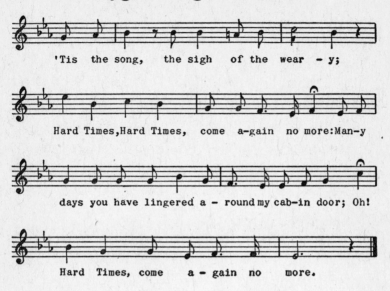

'Tis the song, the sigh of the wear - y;

Hard Times, Hard Times, come a-gain no more: Man-y

days you have lingered a - round my cab-in door; Oh!

Hard Times, come a - gain no more.

In the spring of 1833, Stephen and his mother and Etty made a trip to visit Mrs. Foster's brothers in Augusta, Kentucky, a pleasant village on the bank of the Ohio River. This trip was a delightful adventure for Stephen; for part of it was made aboard the Ohio River packet, the *Napoleon,* the deck hands of which were Negroes from the romantic Deep South.

At night Stephen lay awake in his bunk in the cabin. The cabin was just above the main deck, where the engines and freight were, and where the deck hands and the roustabouts stayed. Among the barrels and boxes, the gear and lines and snubbing posts, the Negroes played their banjos when they were not working, and sang at both work and play. Stephen listened to their voices rising above the noise of the engines, the splashing of

39

the paddle wheels, even above the deep-toned whistle and the clamorous bells. These sounds he stored in his mind, where, by some strange alchemy, they turned into beautiful folk music in the years to come.

During the daytime, the boat tied up every now and then at the wharf of some river town. Stephen watched the roustabouts rolling barrels across the gang-plank, and tossing bundles from hand to hand to the deck. They sang as they worked, always, and it seemed to Stephen that the Negroes made up many of these work songs just as Lieve's people made up the songs they sang in church.

Some of the songs he heard on this trip were gay, nonsense songs. The roustabouts usually sang those on bright warm mornings just after they had received their pay. Other songs were serious, and most of those were sung at night, when the Negroes mourned for their far-off homes and the absent faces dear to them. Some songs were sung just to make the work seem lighter. One of these went:

> "Ain't it dinner?—ho, ho!
> Ain't it dinner?—tell me so!"

With each "Ain't it dinner?" a gang of roustabouts on the wharf swung a heavy crate or box, ready to pitch it to another gang on the deck of the steamboat. With each "ho, ho!" they let go. Pulling, hauling, tossing, lifting—whatever they did, they did in rhythm, and the song went on:

40

"Goin' to leave you! Let's go!
Won't you tell me? Why so!

"If I leave you—ho, ho!
Please don't leave me! Why so!

"Well, let's go! I'm right!
Well, let's go! I'm right!

"Good-bye! I'm gone!
Good-bye! I'm gone!

"To the bottom—ho, ho!
To the bottom—ho, ho!"

They sang ballads describing common pleasures and common sorrows. What the Negroes put into song the white people felt in their hearts was true. So it happened that in their own way the Negroes were singing the joys and sorrows of all, both white and black. Stephen listened and remembered.

After the visit at Augusta, Mrs. Foster took her two children down the river as far as Louisville. On the levee of this busy river port Stephen saw a group of Negroes gathered round one who was dancing. The dancer called his movements the "buck-and-wing." As he danced, shuffling his feet and swinging his arms, he chanted a song to describe his contortions. The spectators grinned and slapped their hands together in time to the wild, barbaric rhythm of the dance. Here is the song of the buck-and-wing dancer:

"Lef' foot dance, right foot res';
Ah shakes mah shoulders an' grins mah bes';
Slides mah shins, an' shuts mah mouf.
Dis am de way we do down Souf!

"Ah lif's mah lef' arm—right arm dips;
Ah shows mah teeth an' smacks mah lips;
'Roll yo' eyes, Black Boy, roll 'em roun';
Kick dat grabble, an' den hoe down!' "

On the trip up river, the steamboat met many rafts floating down stream. The boatmen on these rafts were white. They had songs of their own, some of which were very old and had come across the Atlantic Ocean with an old grandmother in the days of the Colonies. Such a ballad floated across the river to Stephen one night from a lumber raft where the boatmen sat warming themselves around a small fire built on a pile of earth. The words were:

"There is a wild boar in the woods,
Dillum dan diddly, dillum dan diddle,
He eats our flesh and drinks our blood,
Tun a qui quiddle quo quum."

A man on another raft was playing the fiddle. The wild, fast music that he played expressed his own fierce, free spirit. Stephen listened and never forgot the songs and the fiddle music, which were part of the strange magic of the river.

42

All those memories of black and white people singing and dancing, playing the banjo and the fiddle, sank deep into Stephen's mind. Everywhere he went in later years he listened to other humble folk of America singing, just as he had listened to the river men on the Ohio. He came to understand better than anyone else the laughter and tears of a great nation, and when he wrote his own songs later, it seemed to Americans that his songs were not only his but theirs also. It was as if he and a whole nation, like Lieve's people, had made those songs up as they went along.

CHAPTER FOUR

"A PENNY FOR YOUR THOUGHTS"

STEPHEN HALFWAY CLOSED his eyes, stuck out his tongue, and scratched away with pen and ink at the paper before him. The lamp-light fell soft on his dark hair and slender hands. He was writing a letter to his father, making a great effort to spell and think and keep the words from going up hill, all at the same time.

From across the wide dining-room table, Mit with good-natured amusement watched his younger brother. Stephen's mother sat near the hot stove, knitting mufflers to protect her boys from the raw January days. She looked up, caught Mit's smile, and gently shook her head. No one was allowed to hurt another's feelings in the Foster household.

So it was that Mit, keeping a perfectly sober face, read the finished letter that Stephen presented for his final approval before it should be sealed and mailed. He had written:

My Dear Father

I wish you to send me a commic songster for you promised to. if I had my pensyl I could rule my paper. or if I had the

44

money to by Black ink But if I had my whistle I would be so taken with it I do not think I would writ atall. there has been a sleighing party this morning with twenty or thirty cupple. Dr. Bane got home last night and told us Henry was coming out here I wish Dunning would come with hin tell them bothh to try to cone for I should like to see them both most two much to talk about.

I remane your loving son

STEPHEN C. FOSTER.*

Stephen was writing from Youngstown, Ohio. He and Mit and their mother were staying for a time with Etty, who had married Thomas L. Wick of that town. Mr. Foster was in Pittsburgh, working long hours to make a living for his family.

The letter out of the way, Stephen rummaged in a box that contained his books and drawing materials. With drawing pad and water colors he set earnestly to work on a half-finished sketch. It was a scene of delicate beauty Stephen had drawn, a river bank dotted with daisies. Mit stood over him to watch a while, marveling as he often did at the skill of his ten-year-old brother.

Mit more than the others understood the youngest brother. The rest of the family loved Stephen, but, though they were patient with his strange fancies and dreaming ways, they disapproved of them. They did not forbid him to draw or to play his beloved flute, but they did not encourage an artistic temperament which they believed was proper to girls only, if indeed it was proper at all.

* The spelling and punctuation are those of the original.

They tried to understand Stephen, but they could not. The Fosters, like all their neighbors, were too close to early pioneer life, where cutting trees and splitting wood, drawing water, and fighting Indians were more necessary than singing songs. They approved of William, who was an engineer. They were uneasy about Stephen, who dreamed and sang and played his flute and was not interested in arithmetic.

Mit returned with a book to his own chair, but he did not read. In memory, he went back to Stephen's first day at school. The younger brother, just five years old, had walked proudly with Mit to Dame Harvey's school that first morning, with his little primer under his arm.

Seated on a bench with the rest of the beginners, he was set to studying the alphabet under the good Dame's watchful eye. In a few moments he began to grow uneasy, and well he might. For a young child, the alphabet jingles in that absurd primer were a complete puzzle. Under the letter A was the verse:

> "In Adam's fall
> We sinnèd all."

So the jingles went, from bad to worse, until that last letter Z was explained, or perhaps rendered forever mysterious, by the rhyme:

> "Zaccheus he
> Did climb a tree
> His Lord to see."

46

"A Penny for Your Thoughts"

Stephen was becoming terrified. He could make nothing of the mysterious alphabet which he had thought to master on that first day of school. Mit noticed his distress and wanted to help him, but Dame Harvey kept the older brother busy with his own lessons.

When the time came for Stephen to stand up and recite what he had learned, he could bear no more. As Mit told the story later, "his patience gave out, and with a yell like that of a Comanche Indian, he bounded bareheaded into the road, and never stopped running and yelling until he reached home, half a mile away."

Stephen was persuaded to return to Dame Harvey's, but for many years schooldays were a burden to him. It was not until he went to Mr. Stockton's Academy in Allegheny City that he learned to endure cheerfully the long hours of study indoors.

One of the teachers in the Academy had been responsible for the change in Stephen's attitude toward study. This teacher was John Kelly, an amiable Irish gentleman who knew how to be firm without being harsh, and learned without being dull.

Mr. Kelly had been a tutor in the family of Sir Rowland Hill of Birmingham, England, and Dublin, Ireland. Sir Rowland, himself a teacher, had initiated new ideas in discipline and better ways than those generally followed of getting boys to study. Like his former employer, Mr. Kelly did not believe in the prevailing practice of whipping children in school. He used kindness and fair play instead of switches to win the respect of his pupils.

47

Years afterward, the Fosters were to learn more about the pleasant English gentleman for whom their teacher had worked; for it was Sir Rowland who was the first to suggest to the British people that it should be possible to send letters for a penny (two cents) an ounce anywhere in the United Kingdom—with the result that this rate was adopted early in 1840, along with Sir Rowland's idea of a postage stamp. His system was later adopted in America.

When Stephen became a man, he showed his appreciation of Mr. Kelly's kindly help in a poem addressed to the wise teacher of his youth:

> "Old partner of our youthful mirth,
> Thy fruits are scattered o'er the earth;
> And while they bloom scarce mellowed yet,
> The sun that warmed them soon must set.
> But when the final beam is spent
> Thou shalt not lack a monument
> To stand 'mid pride's unmeaning toys
> A landmark of departed joys."

Mit recalled how Stephen had always been restless in the classroom, preferring to walk in the woods and upon the hills by the rivers near his home. Stephen's sensitive ear delighted in the sounds of the countryside. Such soft music as the birds made, or the waters lapping against the river banks, pleased him. Who can say what dreams he dreamed, or what music he heard?

The flowers and the rivers and the trees and the birds

48

all went into the songs which Stephen Foster wrote in the years to come. Once in later life, when he found himself sad and discouraged and longing for the days that would never come again, he wrote a song called *Long-Ago Day,* telling about an old Negro slave who was yearning for the happier time of his youth.

Mit, sitting hunched over his book, glanced up often at Stephen. The younger brother, lost in dreams, remained unaware of the elder brother's sympathetic smile. Stephen will be a musician, Mit was thinking, and in memory he went back to that day, four years before, when Stephen had taught himself to play a flageolet.

The story of that day had often been repeated in the Foster household. Mrs. Foster and Stephen had gone into the music store of Smith & Mellor in Pittsburgh. While his mother talked to the owners of the store, Stephen picked up a flageolet from one of the counters. In a few moments, he had mastered the instrument well enough to play *Hail Columbia* quite creditably. After that surprising feat, it was not long before Stephen was playing the flute with great skill, and with the sweetness and clarity which only the natural musician can achieve.

In much the same way, Stephen taught himself to play the piano, to sing by note, and to write music.

Mit was unusually thoughtful as he remembered these things. He looked at Stephen, who had put away his drawing materials and was sitting with his head inclined to one side as if he were listening to sounds the others

49

could not hear. Mit wondered whether this little brother who neglected his school work for music might some day be a well-known musician.

"Wouldn't it be funny," thought Mit, "if years from now I should be writing a biography of our Stevie—the life of a famous man?" And that is exactly how matters fell out: he did set down his memories of Stephen Foster, by that time the beloved composer of American folk songs.

Mit smiled to himself when he thought of another side of Stephen's character. Stephen, for all his love for the beautiful and quiet scenes around his home, was a real boy. He was no coward, that was a sure thing. He avoided fights, it is true, but he refused to be bullied. In later years, Mit wrote: "Stephen from earliest childhood was noted for his courage, coolness and skill in the combats which continually occur among boys of the same town. . . . He was known as one who must be let alone, and was held in high respect accordingly."

"A penny for your thoughts, Mit," said his mother, smiling at him over her busy knitting needles.

Mit could not tell her what they were. Gentle and patient though she was, she would not understand and probably would worry if she guessed that he believed in Stephen's artistic gifts. So he just said, truthfully enough, "I was thinking of our old teacher, Mr. Kelly, among other people."

CHAPTER FIVE

KEELBOAT MAN FROM THE MASSASSIP'

THE DOCKS AT Pittsburgh were a beehive of activity. So close together that their decks almost touched, the big stern-paddle steamers lined the wharf. There was a sprinkling of smaller craft, too—a barge with a mountain of hides, a keelboat stowing flour and bolt goods and hardware. The roustabouts and deck hands were working like mad, pitching boxes, rolling barrels, carrying sacks. Bosses bawled orders. Stevedores yelled or sang. Dray and carriage horses clattered up and down in front of the warehouses.

Steamboat captains nervously paced the decks of their craft, each one in a fever to shove off—every hour gained meant money in the owners' pockets. All the boats were taking produce to New Orleans, that fickle market where the first cargoes of spring brought the best price and a late cargo might bring nothing at all. The spring rush down the Ohio and the Mississippi rivers was about to begin.

It was nearly noon, but the bright sunshine looked warmer than it was and the sharp breeze, which piled the

51

slushy river ice against the shore, was cold. That is why Stephen sought out a sheltered spot on the sunny side of an old warehouse on the waterfront.

Mrs. Foster and the children had moved from Youngstown back to Allegheny, where Mr. Foster had rented Brother William's house in Gay Alley on the East Common. Once again Stephen's home was near the great Ohio River and its picturesque steamboat traffic.

Stephen should have been in school this bright spring morning. He had started from home with good intentions, as his pile of schoolbooks and lunch pail testified. Or had he? Surely that was a flute sticking through one of the buttonholes of his stout blue jacket, and one was not allowed to bring a flute to school except on "piece-speaking" days.

In the sunny, sheltered corner, Stephen sat down with his boot-covered feet stretched before him and proceeded to eat his lunch. His brown eyes peered over the huge sandwiches as he munched, for he did not want to miss one bit of the animated scene on the levee. He had pushed his cap back at a rakish angle so that he looked quite reckless. Indeed, he was feeling reckless, for he was playing truant, and he knew that he had some form of punishment waiting for him at the end of the day.

His mother would look sad. That was not a pleasant thought, and it made him blink, as if he sought to brush it away with his long lashes.

His lunch eaten, Stephen replaced the lid on his dinner pail and set it carefully on top of his schoolbooks. He

52

ran over to where a grinning black boy was walking amongst the sweating stevedores with buckets of drinking water. Good-naturedly the water boy gave Stephen a drink from one of the dippers. Then Stephen returned to his sunny corner. Taking the flute from beneath his jacket, he began to play.

The high, sweet notes of the flute fell pleasantly on the crisp air. Black men paused in their work to listen, and slapped their thighs in approval. Pilots, captains, and merchants took their cigars from their lips and smiled as they watched the boy.

Stephen was not aware of the interest his music was exciting. Engrossed in his playing, he gazed sidewise along the flute to watch his own fingers skipping about nimbly.

Since the time when as a small boy he had seen a flageolet for the first time and taught himself in less than ten minutes to play a tune on it, Stephen had become an expert flutist. Sitting in the sunshine on the wharf, he played gay dance tunes and sprightly songs with an air of assurance. Graceful waltzes he played, and the wistful folk music of the Negroes. A minstrel ditty. Then something of his own—not a song, just his finger experimenting with pleasing combinations of notes. Sweet playing, remarkably good for a boy who had never had a music lesson in his life.

A bleary-eyed old man shuffled up, rolled a keg to a spot beside Stephen, and sat down heavily. Stephen, still playing, stared over the flute at the queerest person he had ever seen, even on the levee where all classes and conditions of men met and mingled. The old man's face was so wrinkled that it reminded Stephen of a bit of dried apple. He had no hair showing beneath the rim of his tight round cap; so Stephen guessed there would be none above it. He wore a red flannel shirt, soiled and patched, and baggy trousers that looked as if they had been made of tow-sacking. His gnarled old feet were bare, the joints distorted and stiffened by rheumatism.

When Stephen came to the end of the song, the old fellow on the keg clapped his hands together and laughed in a dry, cackling sort of way.

"Purty good, bub! Smartest moosic I've yeared since me and my crew was down to Natchez raisin' a whirl-wind."

"Are you a pilot?" asked Stephen politely.

The question cut the old man's laughter short.

"You wouldn't be aimin' to make fun of a body, would ye, bub? No, I calkilate not, I calkilate not." He answered his own question, for there was shrewdness in his watery eyes and he had been quick to notice Stephen's distress. "No, bub," the man went on. "I ain't never had no truck with them smoke-belchin', steam-spittin' river devils. Hate 'em! Hate 'em wuss nor p'izen, that's what I do!" He spat viciously in the general direction of the steamboats.

"Why do you hate them?" Stephen was curious.

"For why? Huh! Them tea-kittles took th' very vittles outen our mouths, that's what they done! They druv us

54

offen th' river. Mighty few keelboat men left, bub."

"Keelboat? Oh, you mean like that one there?" Stephen pointed out the boat taking on flour and hardware. It had a narrow, sharp-ended hull, decked over to protect the cargo, and inside the gunwales was a runway of plank for the men who used the sweeps and setting poles. No sail or engine would move this boat. Down river she would go, two hard-muscled men at the forty-foot stern sweeps steering a course, other bull-necked, hairy-chested men weaving back and forth at the side sweeps to drive her. Up river the keelboat men would "walk" her with the setting poles, breasting the current with muscle and sinew.

"What'd I say!" The old man spoke vehemently. "Boys nowadays ain't even sure they know a keel when they see one. Sure, that-air is a keel—not as long as some, but she's a keel, all right. Reason I come down today—heerd up town they was a keel loadin' fer N'Orleans. Nawthin' on 'arth I'd ruther be, bub, than a sweep man, ready to take a keel down th' old Massassip'," he added wistfully.

"What do you do now?" Stephen looked pityingly at the old man's rags and bare feet.

"Me? Nawthin', bub, nawthin' a-tall. Live on what I kin pick up, like. Sometimes I git a invite to go a piece down th' river on a raft or su'thin'. Th' men like th' yarns I tell, and they gener'ly give me 'nuff beans and bacon and corn to tide me over a spell. Ye wouldn't think to see me now that I was wunst th' out-fightinest,

55

out-bragginest, out-shootinest alligator-hoss on th' Massassip', would ye now?"

"What's an alligator-horse?" Stephen asked, evading the man's question.

"River man, bub, river man—much at home on th' water as ary pup-eatin' 'gator, an' strong as a hoss when he took holt of th' tow rope an' helped pull a keel up river. A sight to see, sweatin' through their flannel shirts, diggin' their toes into th' bank to git a better holt, cussin' a blue streak. Alligator-hosses!"

Stephen listened attentively as the old man rambled on with his tales of the river in the days before steam. As a boy, this man had walked along the Wilderness Path with Daniel Boone, and with other pioneers he had later pushed farther to the west, into Ohio. He had been a man grown when Tecumseh was organizing the tribes for rebellion in the Indiana Territory.

Lost in a world of dreams and memory, the old man drew for Stephen word-pictures of the motley craft on the Ohio and Mississippi rivers in the first years of the Nineteenth Century: timber rafts from the mountain streams; pirogues built of the trunks of trees hollowed out by burning; broadhorns, so called because of the two curved steering sweeps extending from either side of the square hull like ox horns; the keelboats, swiftest of the oar-propelled craft; New Orleans and Kentucky flatboats, carrying emigrants, their household goods and pigs and chickens, even cows and mules besides; shanty boats, which were the floating homes of the very poor.

Shops and business enterprises of all kinds did not "stay put," the old man explained to Stephen, but went floating about among the freight and passenger boats. There were floating lottery offices, and boats where brokers did business with those wishing to gamble in pork or grain futures. Boats belonging to tinners plied the rivers, tying up at landings along the way to sell tinware or to mend it. Some of the boats were smithies, where horses and oxen were shod and wagons repaired. Some were workshops where axes, scythes, and other edge-tools were made. And there were hundreds of dry-goods boats with cloth and pins and needles and other "Yankee notions" for sale to the settlers' families.

"Th' trip from Pitt to N'Orleans took six weeks," said the old man; "th' trip back took six months."

Then he told Stephen about the man-killing work of taking a keel up river. There were several ways. Sometimes the men poled the boat: digging the sharp setting poles into the bank or the bottom of the river, the crew shoved with all their might to gain a few feet against the current. Sometimes the men walked along the bank, pulling the boat forward with tow ropes. Sometimes they "warped" the boat up stream: One or two men in a small boat would row ahead of the keelboat, select a likely tree, and tie to it the lines they had carried with them. The other end of those lines was retained by the men aboard the keel, who, hand over hand along the ropes, hauled the heavy boat to the tree.

"And now it's all over and done with," sighed the old

57

keelboat man. "Nawthin' but these steam-snorters. *Gentlemen* in lace ruffles steerin' 'em; cheap black labor mannin' 'em. Druv us river men plumb off th' river. Dagnabbed engines. It's agin' natur', that's what it is. Agin' natur'!"

"Where did they go—the river men?" asked Stephen.

"Go? Well, bub, most of 'em's dead. Some of th' younger ones moved on west to th' Missouri, where life's still free an' a man can be a man, 'stid of a dandy with lace ruffles. Ye see, bub, th' life of danger is th' only life fer a keelboater, an' th' Ohio an' Massassip'—Shucks! They're tame as a ladies' boarding house. Steerin' a boat with lace ruffles an' linen! Huh!"

"But you didn't leave," Stephen pointed out.

"No. Ye're right, bub. I didn't leave. Seems like I had to stick to th' old rivers—couldn't move on. Too old, I reckon. Or mebbe I'm jest like one of them orn'ry sawyers that weave around jest under th' surface of th' water. Them trees ain't rooted—they *could* move on, but they don't—they stay in might' near th' same place, year in year out."

The old man reached round and began tugging at something in the back pocket of his shabby breeches. Pulling and hauling, he was finally successful. Stephen's interested eyes watched as he produced a flat, stoppered bottle. Removing the cork, the old man drained off an ounce or so of the amber liquid.

"Corn," he explained, drawing the back of his gnarled hand over his lips. "Corn liquor, bub. Live on it! Reckon it'd be better if I didn't, but it makes ye fergit yer mis'ry. Makes ye fergit. Reckon, though, if I had it to do over agin, bub, I wouldn't touch ary a drap."

The whiskey lent the old man temporary eloquence. His speech was a window opening to permit a little boy to see what an old derelict might once have been.

"Remember that, bub," he went on. "Ye can't do it over agin. No, sir. Ye go down river an' ye' can't warp back up.

"Life is like a river, many ways. Starts out bright an' happy as a purty spring or brook. That's its baby days. Flows on sweet an' gentle, gittin' bigger as other cricks join it. Gits to be a young river, flowin' along peaceful an' nice. Then snags show up an' a rock or two. Goin' ain't so easy any more. Atter a while comes th' falls— rough goin'.

"I reckon you an' me's kinda like th' keelboats on that river, bub. Got to look out sharp fer snags. Got to know how to take th' falls at spring rise. Lots o' things to swamp us—sawyers an' snags an' wood islands an' sudden storms. To git safe to th' sea, we got to *know* that river. We got to look way ahead fer snags. Yep, bub, th' long river windin' to th' sea—that's what life is. Some of us don't never git to be good hands at th' steerin' sweep, neither, an' we git swamped, like as not. Yes, sir, like as not. . . . Pshaw!" he broke off. "Ye ain't interested in snags an sech-like. Wait'll I take another little swig. Then you can give us a tune. What say?"

Stephen kept silent, thinking of the old man's serious

59

talk of the river and life. Much of it he did not understand, but it disturbed him vaguely. Watching the man take his "swig," Stephen lifted his flute to his lips.

It was a jig tune Stephen chose, and when he came to the end of it, the old man chuckled his approval.

"That-air tune is one Mike Fink woulda liked. Mike Fink—he was a red-headed Irishman. Cock o' th' walk, he was, an' no one was atter pluckin' th' feather from his cap, neither."

The old man was in the past again, describing for Stephen the characters of keelboat days on the "Massassip'." The work of the river men was hard, and their play was cruel. They enjoyed such sports as cock-fighting, and they fought each other for the love of battle. Their speech was a curious mixture of ugliness and beauty and they were fond of wild exaggeration and grotesque comparisons. "I'm the son of lightning!" one would boast, and another would pick a fight with, "I'm death and destruction! No rock can kill me, no ocean is deep enough to drown me, and I can drink up the river!"

Wherever there was danger you could be sure to find the river man. All his life he looked for adventure and trouble, and was seldom disappointed in his search. Money was valuable to him only because with it he could go from place to place in search of excitement. He had no home but the river—and on the river he usually met the violent death which seemed ever to be his destiny.

"On th' way down stream," said the old man, "we used

60

ter sing. Right purty, too, of a moonlight night, layin'
on our backs lookin' up at th' sky. One of th' songs I
reckylect was this one." In a tipsy voice he sang:

"The boatman is a lucky man,
 No one can do as the boatman can,
 The boatman dance, and the boatman sing,
 The boatman do 'most any old thing.
　Hi-O, away we go,
　Floating down the river on the O-hi-O."

Stephen was day-dreaming and heard no more. He
wondered if the boatmen's song had been made up as
they went along. It was a happy-go-lucky tune. Some day,
he decided, he would write a ballad for the roustabouts
and the deck hands and the boatmen to sing. Years later
he did write such a song for the men of the river. He
wrote, too, a song about the steamboat named the *Glendy
Burk*—a jolly tune, with verses that picture all the color
and the bustle and the pathos and the gaiety of the river:

THE GLENDY BURK*

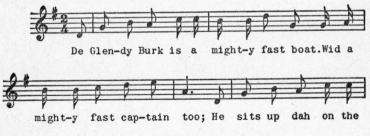

De Glen-dy Burk is a　might-y fast boat.Wid a

might-y　fast cap-tain　too; He　sits up　dah　on the

*The spelling and punctuation are those of the original.

61

hur-ri-cane roof And he keeps his eye on de

crew. I can't stay here, for dey work too hard; I'm

bound to leave dis town; I'll take my duds and

tote 'em on my back When de Glen-dy Burk comes down.

Chorus

Ho! for Lou'-si-an-a! I'm

bound to leave dis town; I'll take my duds and

tote 'em on my back When de Glen-dy Burk comes down.

Second Verse

De Glendy Burk has a funny old crew,
And dey sing de boatman's song;
Dey burn de pitch and de pine knot too,
For to shove de boat along.
De smoke goes up and de ingine roars
And de wheel goes round and round,
So fair you well! for I'll take a little ride
When de Glendy Burk comes down.

62

Keelboat Man from the Massassip'

Third Verse

I'll work all night in de wind and storm,
  I'll work all day in de rain,
Till I find myself on de levy-dock
  In New Orleans again.
Dey make me mow in de hay field here
  And knock my head wid de flail,
I'll go wha dey work wid de sugar and de cane
  And roll on de cotton bale.

Fourth Verse

My lady love is as pretty as a pink,
  I'll meet her on de way.
I'll take her back to de sunny old south
  And dah I'll make her stay.
So dont you fret my honey dear,
  OH! dont you fret Miss Brown.
I'll take you back 'fore de middle of de week
  When de Glendy Burk comes down.

The sun was setting when Stephen left the wharf. The old man had begged and been granted passage for a few miles down river on the keelboat.

Stephen's mind was awhirl with the day's adventure. He was uneasy, too, dreading to face his parents. Now that it was too late for regrets, he was sorry he had stolen a holiday. Wearily he plodded across the bridge towards the lights of Allegheny. Snags in the river. . . .

CHAPTER SIX

"WHEN I WAS A BOY"

IT WAS IN the summer of 1837, the year of a serious financial panic in the United States. The President, Mr. Van Buren, had called a special session of Congress to consider relief for the many people who were out of work and hungry. Starving people in New York had rioted for food.

Stephen's father was struggling to provide the money to buy bread for his own family. With the help of Brother William they were keeping their heads above water. Mr. Foster wrote in one of his letters: "Such times you never saw—the banks refuse specie, and nothing but shinplasters for change." By shinplasters he meant the paper money in small denominations under a dollar that were then being issued by private bankers and companies.

Mr. Foster often thought longingly of earlier days, when, it seemed to him, there had been richer opportunity for poor young men to make a start in life. So it was that in the evening hours before lamp-lighting time he sat on the veranda of his home on East Common, in Allegheny City, telling Dunning and Mit and Stephen tales of frontier life before the War of 1812 and since.

64

"When I Was a Boy"

The Fosters were an old family and a proud, and their history was like the figures embroidered on a tapestry, the tapestry which was the history of America. Mr. Foster spoke of the family in Colonial days, and though the boys had heard the story many times they enjoyed it once again, like a friendly book that has lost none of its interest for having been read to tatters.

Mr. Foster spoke of his grandfather, Alexander Foster, who had been an emigrant from Londonderry, Ireland, and had settled more than a hundred years before in Lancaster County, Pennsylvania.

"He lived and his children were born in the Conestoga Valley, Lancaster," said Mr. Foster. "In that valley the first Conestoga wagons were built. Some day a book will be written to tell how great a part in our history was played by those early wagons of the turnpikes, built in the old blacksmith shops of Lancaster."

"You used to run a line of Conestogas between here and Philadelphia, didn't you?" inquired Mit, who had a flair for business.

"Yes," said Mr. Foster. "I helped organize a freighting company right after the War of 1812. Like so many of my business ventures," he added sadly, "it did not make money. For one thing, the turnpikes were in bad shape. After a rain or a wet snow, the wagons floundered in soft ruts as deep as their wheels were high, delaying the schedules and wearing thin the patience of the drivers. The steep grade over the Alleghenies required doubling the teams of mules; that meant heavy added expense.

"Those mules, though!" The pioneer, not the business-man, in Mr. Foster was speaking. "Those smooth-flanked mules with their steel muscles working under the tan and black hides! They were the best to be had. It was a sight to see a train of our wagons. Iron-shod wheels, canvas-covered tops, blue and red flaring beds. They looked like bright-colored river bateaux. Swaying and creaking with loads of hardware and dry goods and furniture piled to the very top of the tarpaulins, they crept up hill. The mule-skinners walked alongside, yelling and cracking long blacksnake whips. At the top of the grade the mules were rested. When the drivers climbed to their seats, the teams were started down hill. The wagons gained speed rapidly, until they were plunging down the road, taking the curves at a dangerous pace, with the brake-blocks screeching against the iron rims of the wheels. A hand-some sight!"

Beyond the East Common at that moment, on the road leading to the pleasant camping grounds at The Point, a team of horses was pulling a canvas-covered Conestoga wagon in the thickening dusk.

"Look!" exclaimed Dunning excitedly. "There's an-other one. Emigrants to the Missouri country. They've been going by all week, more and more of them."

"That's because of the Panic," said Mr. Foster. "Poor souls—most of them have lost their homes and their farms. They hope to make new homes far away from banks and mortgages. Well, good luck to them—good luck and courage and strength! They will need all three."

"When I Was a Boy"

Faintly the creaking of wheels reached the boys and their father, and a few notes of a mournful song. The driver to the west country was singing to forget his weariness while his tired horses plodded toward the river and the promise of feed bags and rest.

The little group on the porch watched the wagon out of sight. Mr. Foster was thinking of the early days, when Pittsburgh had been the last outpost of civilization in the West. Now the frontier had moved on to faraway St. Louis. Soon, he reflected, it would move again. Who could say? Perhaps the wagons would follow the route of Lewis and Clark to the Oregon Territory, and populous cities might spring up along the Pacific coast. A freighting company would be formed— He shook his head. He was dreaming again. Cross the Rocky Mountains, the Great American Desert, and the Sierra Nevadas in wagons? No. It would not be done—not by many, anyway. He could not know that within ten years thousands of Conestogas, or "prairie schooners" as they came to be called, would be making a well-traveled highway of the Oregon Trail.

Dunning dreamed of adventure among Indian tribes as he watched the swaying wagon beyond East Common. Pioneers traveling westward would see the plains Indians who dwelt with the buffalo. Moving from hunting ground to hunting ground beyond the Mississippi, they used horses and dogs to pull drags made of poles, on which tents and the old people and the babies were lashed for the long marches. Hundreds and hundreds of braves

67

and squaws and horses and dogs moving across the plains in a cloud of dust. Trappers returning from the land beyond the great Mississippi often came east as far as Pittsburgh, and their tales had set Dunning's heart longing for adventure in the wilds.

Mit thought of the distant lands where the emigrants would settle. New farms, new houses, new stores. There would have to be stores, he mused, stores with barrels of apples and calico bolt goods and pink rock-sugar. It would be fun to own a store like that, Mit thought. He would sell candles, and shoes that came in barrels, rights and lefts tied together by the laces, axes for chopping trees to make log cabins, pins and needles, too, if the traveling peddlers did not come right away with these notions in their carts. Mit's heart longed for enterprise in the new, raw land.

Stephen listened to the mournful song of the driver and drew a little closer to his father. The music made him feel lonely and sad, and he was glad when he could no longer distinguish the notes from the whisper of the soft breeze stirring the leaves of the poplars. Content to remain at home, Stephen even in imagination shrank from following the lonely adventurer and his song into a harsh wilderness.

Mit broke the silence and ended their woolgathering. "So we've lived for more than a hundred years in Pennsylvania, we Fosters," he said wonderingly.

"Yes." His father nodded. "Though we Fosters often stray far, we quite as often return to our own hearthstones in Pennsylvania, which has been our home since my father's day. He left his home in Virginia to go soldiering for seven long weary years during the Revolutionary War. He was at Yorktown when Cornwallis surrendered. As soon as he was mustered out, however, he emigrated with some of the Scotch-Irish families of Virginia to western Pennsylvania. He settled in Canonsburg, nineteen miles from Pittsburgh. There he married Ann Barclay, a relative of the Rowans and the Barclays of Kentucky. It was Judge Rowan who built the beautiful plantation home of Federal Hill at Bardstown, Kentucky."

"Federal Hill is where Charlotte used to visit, isn't it?" asked Dunning.

"Yes. Charlotte was always a welcome guest at Federal Hill." Mr. Foster spoke wistfully. "Your mother has her dear letters yet, telling of the good times she had in that old Kentucky home."

The sadness which always followed mention of the gentle sister who had died settled on the boys and their father. Stephen, who had no memory of his sister, was distressed because the others were sad. Seeking to change the subject, he suggested, "Tell us about when you were a boy, Pa. When you worked for the store and made trips to New Orleans."

"Oh, ho, Stevie! So it's my old blood-and-thunder tales you want to hear. When I was a boy! A long time ago it seems, too. Well, when I was a boy, just sixteen years old, I came here to Pittsburgh—a mighty different Pittsburgh from what it is today. That was in 1796. No coal had been mined, and there were no factories.

"My job for the firm of Beelen and Denny was to take charge of their flatboats loaded with flour, furs, and pork to be sold in New Orleans. All the way down the Ohio and the Mississippi those boats were taken by rough crews of oarsmen under my watchful eye.

"In New Orleans I sold our cargoes for money, or possibly exchanged them for sugar and coffee and other products of Louisiana and the West Indies. These exchange products had to be poled up river to some market where they could be sold.

"If I got money right away in New Orleans, I usually took ship for Philadelphia to buy goods imported from Europe. Packets out of New Orleans sailed through the Gulf of Mexico into southern waters near Cuba, passed north through the Straits of Florida, and so up the coast past Georgia, the Carolinas, and Virginia to Philadelphia. On one of those trips I was very nearly captured by pirates."

"You never told us that before!" Dunning sat up eagerly. "Are you joking?"

"Joking? I should say not! I'll tell you about it. Early one morning, when the mists from bayou and river and sea began to lift from the Delta, the ship on which I had engaged passage to Philadelphia put out of the harbor of New Orleans. We were three hours on our course before the breeze had entirely dispersed the low-lying clouds. We moved slowly over the water, for there was little

70

wind. Every inch of canvas was spread to catch the light airs, and I was walking up and down the deck thinking to myself what a fine sight we must be, like some great sea bird with outspread wings, when to the south and west there appeared sails on the horizon. The breeze was more in their favor than in ours, and it was soon evident that there were three ships and that they were following a course which would bring them athwart our bows.

"The captain was on the bridge observing the craft through his glass. We passengers on deck were anxious, for we knew as well as the captain that pirates infested the southern waters. By noon our worst fears were realized. Three rakish craft displaying no flag were bearing down upon us.

"I had a sort of gone feeling in my stomach, as I watched the ships drawing closer. I had heard of West Indian pirates making people walk the plank. After plundering a ship, they would burn it. Many a good ship had disappeared in this way, with none left to tell the story.

"Our captain, on seeing the pirate craft closing in, simply gave orders to reef sail and lay to. We thought him a very great coward; for naturally we concluded that he was going to give up the ship without a struggle. One of the cabin passengers said as much, and suggested that we at least put up a fight. The packet mounted two small cannon, and there were pistols and muskets and a goodly store of powder and shot.

71

" 'Give the order to fight, sir,' said this passenger to the captain, 'and we are with you to the last man.'

" 'I shall give the order to fight when it is necessary,' replied the skipper coldly, and turned his back.

"There was a good deal of grumbling at this speech, but, since the captain's word was law on board ship, we just watched the pirate craft uneasily. What was our horror when we saw one of the ships lowering a boat. Fear stalked our decks when five of the black-browed buccaneers, with knives and pistols in their belts, boarded us. We judged them to be Creoles, and thought of all the horrible tales we had heard of Lafitte and his men.

"At that moment we had to admire our captain. Standing with his hands behind his back, his stout legs planted firmly on the deck, he watched the intruders with scornful eyes. He showed not the least sign of fear. We even got the impression that he had some joke of his own; for the corners of his mouth twitched as if from suppressed laughter.

"The pirate in command left his fellows by the rail and strode up to the captain. In English with a strong French accent he said, 'We have ordaire to search your ship.'

" 'Whose orders?' Our captain was as cold as ice in his manner toward the Creole.

" 'The ordaire of our captaine,' the rogue said impudently.

" 'If I were you, I shouldn't search,' said our captain.

"The pirate was puzzled. 'You are ver' bold man,' he said finally, 'to take that tone weeth me.'

72

" 'Mebbe,' said our Yankee captain.

"The pirate looked about him uneasily. 'You expect another ship along, *non?*'

" 'Mebbe.'

" 'So. Ship from Spain, eh, maybe?'

" 'Mebbe.'

" 'Maybe you try to make a fool of us, too, eh? Maybe no ship come?'

" 'Mebbe.'

"The two men sized each other up. Our captain stared the pirate down, and the Creole turned suddenly on his heel. With a word of command to those waiting at the rail, he swung on the boarding ropes to the boat below. Swiftly they rowed back to their ship. Several men from the other ship rowed over to join them. We could tell they were holding a council of war.

"Our captain lifted his spy-glass and gazed back along the sea lane we had traveled. He ignored the enemy.

"The pirates held off. Long minutes passed—minutes of fear and tension on board the packet, minutes of indecision on the pirate craft. About mid-afternoon, what was our surprise to see a ship rise slowly above the horizon at our back. The buccaneers watched that ship as anxiously as we, and when they saw that she flew the flag of Spain at her masthead, they crowded on all sail and left us in a hurry.

"The cabin passenger who had spoken to the captain before, spoke up again. 'Tell us, sir—did you *know* the

Spanish ship was due? And if so, sir, how in the name of the seven devils of the deep did ycu know?'

"Our captain eyed the excited passenger amusedly. 'Mebbe I didn't,' he said. Then he went into his cabin and shut himself up for a long time with his maps and charts."

"Whew! Those were wild days, all right." There was awe in Dunning's voice.

"Wild and rough," agreed his father. "If the journey home by sea was dangerous, the land route from Louisiana was even more so. Sometimes there would be no ship ready to sail from New Orleans and none expected to leave for a month or two. In that case, I joined one of the groups of traders banded together for protection and went home horseback along the dreaded Natchez Trace and Tennessee Path.

"On the land route one had white outlaws to fear as well as Indians. Murrell and his bandits had their headquarters near Cave-in-Rock on the Ohio, but they ranged all through the dark forests, even into the dismal Louisiana swamps, where huge cypress trees stood in pools of water black as ink. Into these forests the sun could not penetrate. It made one jumpy—the darkness and the soft splashing sounds. One was conscious of the stealthy life, animal and human, lurking always just out of sight."

"Who was Murrell?" asked Mit.

"Murrell was a notorious outlaw—a remarkable but vicious man. He organized a group of cutthroats numbering more than a thousand men. He called his horrible gang the Mystic Clan. They were placed all up and down the Ohio River, and along the lonely land trails, where they made a business of horse-stealing, Negro-stealing, highway robbery, and wholesale murder. By the way, I saw Murrell once."

"Pa! You never told us that either." Dunning sounded so reproachful that Mr. Foster and Mit and Stephen laughed heartily.

"Well, I did see him. A bunch of us were camped one night after a hard day's riding. All of a sudden into the circle of the campfires stalked a tall man, as bold as you please. It was Murrell. He was dressed in one of his favorite disguises, the garb of a country parson. He was a handsome man in a hawklike way. He made no bones about who he was. He had no fear that we would make trouble for him, since we were well aware that a signal from him would bring his henchmen like jackals out of the forests. He did not trouble himself to rob us, either; it seems he was 'laying low' as the result of some vicious crime."

"He *was* a renegade, wasn't he!" breathed Mit.

"A monster. In his parson's dress he would ride into some pioneer settlement, gaining the confidence of men, women, and children with his soft speech and pious praying, waiting until he found out which family had received cash for the summer planting. Then a few swift blows with an ax or a knife, not even sparing the children, and Murrell was gone, his booty in his belt, more innocent blood on his conscience—if he had a conscience.

75

"There was no mercy in him. It is a terrible thing to see a man without pity, a terrible thing." Mr. Foster sighed. "Strange that such a man should almost have brushed shoulders with the great and gentle Daniel Boone."

"Did you know Daniel Boone?" asked Stephen, who had already heard stories of the famous woodsman who had guided the early settlers into Kentucky.

"I talked to him once," said Mr. Foster. "The old wilderness scout was getting gray when I saw him, but he was as straight as a pine tree and sturdy as an oak. I remember his keen eyes, and how they seemed to look right through a man. I had heard all the stories about how he had been captured and tortured by the Indians, how he had always found a way to escape, and how in spite of all the suffering he had endured at the hands of the redskins he had never sought vengeance. I guess I expected Boone to tell about those experiences, and about his long hunts when he was alone in the forests for two years at a time. He didn't mention those things. It was as if he considered them not worth mentioning. He spoke instead of the trees and the scurrying animals and the sound of axes biting into green timber. His mind was filled with the worship of silent places.

"As a boy, he had learned to follow the Indian trails. His sharp eyes read the trail as if it had been an open book. Had an Indian passed along it with moccasined feet? Or had it been one of the settlers? He could tell you. He knew the calls of the turkeys and the chattering of squirrels, and he could tell when these calls were made not by the creatures of the forest but by Indians who imitated them in order to signal to other members of the tribe. Forest sounds spoke to him of concealed enemies, apprised him of game near at hand. Of all the great hunters, he was the greatest. Yet in spite of a lifetime of danger, hardship, and conflict, he was of all gentle men, I think, the gentlest."

The little group on the porch fell silent, thinking of the bewildering pageant of the early days. The dusk had long since given way to darkness, and the fireflies had come out to show their lamps in the warm summer air. From afar off, below The Point, a steamboat whistle sounded faintly on the breeze.

"Ah, when I was a boy," said Mr. Foster, "there were no steamboats."

CHAPTER SEVEN

MINSTRELS IN TOWN!

THE FOSTERS HAD moved again. They had left the house in Gay Alley to live in Poland, Ohio, not far from Stephen's Uncle Struthers. Thus it was that one summer's afternoon in 1839 found Mrs. Foster busy with the hundred-and-one tasks which always go along with settling into a new home. Stephen came bursting into the kitchen, where she was scrubbing cupboards. He was out of breath from hurrying, and his dark eyes burned with excitement.

"Well, Stevie? What on earth is the matter? And where is Mit?"

"He's coming. He stayed to watch the parade, but I hurried home to ask if we might go."

"What are you talking about? Go where, child? And what parade?" Mrs. Foster hardly knew whether to be amused at the excited boy or out of patience with him.

"The minstrel parade. The minstrels are in town—Christy's Minstrels—and they are going to give a show tonight!"

Mrs. Foster looked with troubled eyes at the eager child. "Oh, Stevie, you know I don't approve of the

78

theater. Rough, rowdy crowds. The audience as coarse as the actors."

Stephen's disappointment showed in his sensitive face so keenly that Mrs. Foster's kind heart was touched.

"We shall ask your father, Stevie," she said.

Stephen was instantly happy again; for he was already sure that he and Mit might go. Pa would say, "Oh, let them go. As long as they know how to behave themselves like gentlemen, they cannot be hurt by the company around them."

At supper Mr. Foster did say something very much like that, and Mrs. Foster smiled agreement. Two very happy boys walked to town early in order to get a seat as close to the stage as possible.

The barnlike theater was hot and stuffy, for it was midsummer. There was a large audience, mostly men; and, as Mrs. Foster had said, it was a rough crowd—iron workers, blacksmiths, river men, shipyard workers, roustabouts. They talked loudly of the rough, hard work they did, and as they talked they did a good deal of spitting; for most of them were chewing tobacco. American theaters of that day were all very much the same; so Mit and Stephen were used to the crude manners of the audience. Besides, they were too much excited watching for the red curtain to slide back to notice their neighbors.

Minstrel shows were fairly new at that time. The boys had seen one or two performances by comedians with blackened faces, but these had been short comic interludes between the acts of regular plays. Stephen and Mit had seen Daddy Rice himself, singing and dancing. Both boys knew the story behind Rice's famous Jim Crow song, first of the real blackface minstrel ditties.

Daddy Rice had been walking along a street in Cincinnati (or perhaps Louisville), so the story went, when he heard an old Negro singing a song with the refrain:

"Turn about an' wheel about an' do jis so,
 An' ebery time I turn about I jump Jim Crow."

Rice, who was a great showman, was struck with the idea of dressing in patched clothing and singing the Jim Crow song at his next stop, which was to be Pittsburgh.

There was in Pittsburgh at that time a Negro named Cuff who earned his living by carrying the trunks of passengers from the steamboats to the hotels. He also would open his mouth for boys to pitch pennies into it at three paces' distance; he was allowed to keep all the coins that went into his mouth. Daddy Rice offered to pay Cuff if he would lend his worn clothes as a costume for the Jim Crow act. Cuff agreed, but since he had no other clothes, he had to hide behind some stage scenery in the wings to wait for the act to end.

When Daddy Rice appeared on the stage, there was a ripple of laughter in the audience. Rice had blackened his face with burnt cork and had painted a ring of white about his mouth. When he began to sing the Jim Crow song and to dance with big slapping feet, the audience went wild with joy.

80

Minstrels in Town!

In the midst of the performance came the whistle of a steamboat. Poor Cuff, hiding without his clothes, was in agony lest he should lose a chance of making a few cents carrying trunks. He could not wait for the act to be finished. He crept as near the stage as he dared and called: "Massa Rice, Massa Rice. Must have my clo'se! Steamboat's coming!"

The audience heard Cuff call. They laughed and applauded until the curtains had to be closed. So it was that the first minstrel performance was given, a type of show which was to become more popular than any other kind in America, and even in England.

After a while the oil lamps on the stage were lighted, and those in the auditorium turned off. There was a hushing of voices. The red curtains rolled away from each other.

On the stage, in a semicircle, fifteen men sat in cane-bottomed chairs. At the back, center, was an important-looking man in full evening dress, with a gold watch chain shining against his waistcoat.

"He's called the Interlocutor," Stephen whispered to Mit.

On either side of the man in black evening dress were ranged men in purple coats and yellow silk trousers. The two end men, who sat nearest the footlights, were dressed in outlandish stripes in every color of the rainbow, and one wore a yellow wig, and the other a purple. All except

81

the Interlocutor had black faces with white circles about their mouths, the style set by Daddy Rice.

As the curtain opened they were making a great racket. Each man was playing some instrument for dear life. The Interlocutor played the violin. The men in purple coats played banjos. The banjo was an appropriate instrument for black-face comedians; it had been invented in America by the Negro slaves from Africa.

The man with the yellow wig played a set of "bones"—real horse ribs that he clacked together in time with the music. These dry and seasoned bones were also appropriate, for cannibal Negroes in Africa had probably thus made merry with the shinbones of their latest victim. In the show, the man with the horse ribs was always called "Bones."

The man in the purple wig had a tambourine to bang and shake. This end-man was always called "Tambo."

The music they played with such a will was *Zip Coon* or *Turkey in the Straw*. They sang the chorus:

> "Old Zip Coon is a very learned scholar,
> Old Zip Coon is a very learned scholar,
> Old Zip Coon is a very learned scholar,
> And he plays upon de banjo Cooney in de holler."

Stephen and Mit sat on the edges of their chairs, their eyes as round as silver dollars as they watched the lively scene.

Bones went "clack-clacky-clack" with the horse ribs, throwing them up in the air and catching them expertly in time to the gay tune. He performed miracles, it seemed to the two boys. Sometimes he threw one of the bones in the air and caught it behind his back just in time to bring in his "clack" at the right place.

Meanwhile Tambo was going through all sorts of gyrations. Biff . . . Bang . . . Rattle . . . Whirr. . . . Up in the air went the hoop with its sheepskin cover and silvery metal pieces. Down it came, and he caught it under his chair, making believe that he almost dropped it. Up in the air it went again. This time it came down behind his back. Suddenly he was thumping it with chin, elbows, and knees. All at once, there were two tambourines, then three, and he was juggling them in the air.

Plink . . . plunk . . . plink . . . plunk. . . . These were the banjos.

The music rose to a frenzy of sound. The men in the audience stamped their feet to the catchy rhythm. The walls and rafters shook. Stephen sat straight and still for fear of missing one little bit of this glorious noise. His heart pounded, and his breath came short. Minstrel shows were always to affect him thus, even after he was a man grown. The smell of coal-oil from the lamps, the gaudy color of the costumes, the noise and the music, the black faces and the good humor of the performers—these were always dear to him, and for these troupes of traveling minstrels in America he wrote some of his best songs.

The music ended abruptly. The Interlocutor was instantly on his feet.

"Well, Mr. Bones," he said to the man in the yellow wig, "how do you feel this evening?"

"To tell de truf," said Bones, imitating the dialect of the southern Negro, "I feels jes' lak a piece o' Pittsburgh coal, that's what I does."

"You feel like a piece of Pittsburgh coal? How is that?"

"Pretty black," Bones snapped back. Stephen and Mit and the men in the audience laughed uproariously at the simple joke.

The dialogue continued, with rapid crossfire between Bones and the Interlocutor, Tambo and the Interlocutor, or Bones and Tambo.

Tambo took out a tablet and pencil and began to write industriously.

"What are you doing there, Tambo?" asked the Interlocutor.

"I'se doin' mah 'rithmetic, Mr. Interlocutor."

"Well, I'm glad to see you so interested in getting an education, Tambo. Here is a problem for you. Let's see if you can give me the correct answer. If I had three apples, and your sister took two, how many would I have left?"

Tambo looked worried. "If you had three apples, and mah sister took two? Huh! You don' know mah sister! She'd take 'em all, and you wouldn't have *none* lef'!"

"You seem to be having a great deal of difficulty, Tambo. Here, I have a book that will help you. It will do half your work."

84

"Give me two of 'em, Mr. Interlocutor," said Tambo.

"I'm disgusted with you, Tambo. I'll bet Bones here has a lot more book-learning. How are you in history, Bones?" The Interlocutor turned to the other end-man.

Bones puffed himself up boastfully. "I is *good*, Mr. Interlocutor. In fac', I is mighty nigh perfec'!"

"Well, we'll test you. Let's see if you know the English kings. Who came after Henry VIII?"

"Edward VI."

"Who came after Edward?"

"Queen Mary."

"Who followed Mary?"

"De little lamb."

Then came more joking, more songs, a clog dance to the tune of *Root, Hog, or Die,* and a grand "walk-around"—and the curtain closed on the First Part.

Next came the "Olio," an act before the curtain to give the performers back-stage a chance to change scenery and costumes for the Second Part.

The act on this night consisted of a comic speech. One of the players, in the tall hat and gaudy waistcoat of the cheap politician, made an election speech.

"Ladies and Gentlemen," he began. "Elect me to office, and I shall see to it that this town gets a canal. I'll see to it that you good people have a canal if I have to steal the Erie Canal and carry it in on my back. We must have a canal. Without a canal, we cannot have canal boats. What an unthinkable catastrophe!

"A canal will bring to this prosperous countryside

hundreds, nay, thousands of low bridges. Passengers standing on the deck of a canal boat find no difficulty in cracking their heads on low bridges. Cracking heads in this fashion is the great National Pastime! It is being done on every canal in the country. We are, gentlemen, behind the times. And without a canal, we shall remain in our present state of blighted ignorance. Think of it, gentlemen! The bumps and bruises of progress will be absent from the skulls of the citizens of Pittsburgh." . . . So he went on with pleasant satire about crowded sleeping quarters on board the canal packets, the hard shelves that served as beds, and the thin sheets that were called blankets.

He concluded with, "Elect me, gentlemen! I assure you, you can do no worse!" He took a bow or two, and the curtain opened on the Second Part.

Mr. Christy had chosen an Africanized version of a familiar English play for the Second Part or "afterpiece":

Two Negro men lived in a boardinghouse. One worked at his job as waiter in an all-night restaurant from sun-down to sun-up. The other worked as a whitewasher from sun-up to sun-down. Why, thought old Aunty B., their landlady, should she waste two rooms on these men? She decided to rent them the same room; for, since one was gone all night and the other all day, she saw no way for them to find out the deception. In this manner she figured she could collect two rentals for the one room, since each man would think he was renting a room for himself alone.

So it was arranged, and for a while all went well. Of course, the two men met on the stairs occasionally, but each thought the other lived in Aunty B.'s attic.

Mr. Cox, the whitewasher, began to get suspicious, however, when he discovered his supplies being used up faster than was reasonable. At first he thought it was Aunty B. who took them, and he accused her, saying:

"I'd just like to draw your 'tention to de fact (widout any idee ob hurtin' your feelin's) dat de last peck ob coal dat I brought home goes away amazin' fast!"

Aunty B.: De lord a massy, Mr. Cox!

Cox: Yes, an' it ain't on'y de coal—but dat two-cent candle dat I bort free weeks ago—and a quarter-pound ob sugar, de brown kind—and a box of brimstone matches—and a bottle of skeedam snaps wot I take for my cold—all dese tings hab got de consumption mighty bad, and is fallin' away as fast as possible!"

Aunty B. was able to quiet Mr. Cox's suspicions, and he went to work. In a few moments, however, she had to begin all over again with Mr. Box, who returned to his room and began to complain of missing *his* supplies. Mr. Box finally went grumbling off to bed, and Aunty B., feeling that she had already done a full day's work, went off to her household duties.

Pretty soon the unexpected happened. Cox, having been given a holiday by his employer, came back to his room. He did not see Box on the bed because of a screen around it, but the audience did, and they roared with delight.

87

Then began a series of amusing mix-ups. Finally Box and Cox discovered each other. They began to argue wildly about whose room it was.

Cox: Who is you, colored man?

Box: Dat's jes de berry question I was gwine to ax you. Who is *you?*

Cox: What you want here?

Box: Dat's jes what I was gwine to ax you—wot does *you* want?

Cox (aside to the audience): It's de waiter.

Box (aside to the audience): It's de whitewasher.

Cox: Go back to your attic whar you belongs, colored man!

Box: My attic? Guess you better say *your* attic!

And so the argument went on until they called old Aunty B. She had to confess. Crying, she went out to get another room ready. While she was gone, the two men discovered that they were twin brothers separated in childhood. When poor Aunty B. returned, they were laughing together. They refused to take separate rooms, and so affairs were just as they were in the beginning— as matters generally are after an argument.

With Box and Cox settled in a way to satisfy the audience, the whole troupe came out to sing one last song, and the curtain closed for the last time.

It had been an important evening for Stephen. Years later he wrote many songs for the same Mr. Christy who played in *Box and Cox.* Most of the Stephen Foster songs that are sung and loved today were written for just such black-faced minstrels as Bones and Tambo and the banjo-

players. Here is one of the most famous of the songs
written for the minstrels:

OLD FOLKS AT HOME*

Way down u-pon the Swa-nee rib-ber,

Far, far a-way, Dere's wha my heart is

turn-ing eb-ber, Dere's wha de old folks stay.

All up and down de whole cre-a-tion, Sad-ly I

roam, Still long-ing for de old plan-ta-tion,

And for de old folks at home.

Chorus

All de world am sad and drear-y,

Eb-ry where I roam,

Oh! dark-eys how my heart grows wear-y

Far from de old folks at home.

* The spelling and punctuation are those of the original.

He Heard America Sing

Second Verse

All round de little farm I wandered
    When I was young,
Den many happy days I squandered,
    Many de songs I sung.
When I was playing wid my brudder
    Happy was I—
Oh! take me to my kind old mudder,
    Dere let me live and die.

Third Verse

One little hut among de bushes,
    One dat I love,
Still sadly to my mem'ry rushes,
    No matter where I rove.
When will I see de bees a-humming
    All round de comb?
When will I hear de banjo tumming
    Down in my good old home?

CHAPTER EIGHT

UNCLE STRUTHERS

OF ALL STEPHEN FOSTER's childhood memories, perhaps the most pleasant were of his Uncle Struthers, who had a farm at Poland, Ohio. Stephen visited him many times. Once he spent a whole summer with this uncle, who was past eighty when Stephen was just a little boy.

Uncle Struthers had been an Indian fighter and frontiersman in the days when Ohio was peopled mainly by scouts and hunters. Among the earliest settlers was Mr. Struthers, with his wife, who was the sister of Stephen's father. With several brave families they had dared the dangers of the wilderness. Selecting a likely spot, the men of the newly formed community had set to work felling trees to make log houses. They had cleared a space for a corn-field. With their long rifles always close to them they had built their houses, planted their crops, and constructed rail fences. And they had gone hunting for deer, wild turkey, and other game almost in their back yards.

The genial old fellow still lived in a log house, roomy and comfortable, but he had enlarged his fields, built barns and pigpens, increased his crops. He had a yard full of chickens, and some turkeys, the tame kind in these tamer days. And he had some dogs.

Uncle Struthers' dogs were not just ordinary dogs. They were hounds, brought up from Kentucky where they had been bred to hunt. 'Possum hounds, Uncle Struthers called them. They were beautiful creatures, with long flapping ears and glossy coats.

When Stephen was thirteen, he went to spend the summer months on the farm at Poland. Uncle Struthers met Stephen and his mother with the surrey to take them from town to the farm. Stephen was allowed to drive. Holding the reins in both his hands, he slapped them gently on the mare's fat back, and she was off at a brisk trot through the lane bordered with wild plum and choke-cherry.

They were soon arrived at Uncle Struthers' rambling old house. Taking off her bonnet before she was fairly across the threshold, Mrs. Foster immediately set to work tidying up. Because his wife was dead and he lived alone in the house, Uncle Struthers was pretty careless with his housekeeping.

While his uncle unhitched the mare and led her to the south pasture, Stephen explored the farm. The house sat on a pleasant hill, which sloped down on one side to a mossy brook where ferns and violets grew. Beyond the brook were the fields of corn and wheat. Nearer the house was a kitchen garden with onions, turnips, potatoes, beets, beans, and tomatoes. All of these would be eaten except the tomatoes, which were purely ornamental, because in those days tomatoes—called "love-apples"—were considered poisonous by many people.

There was a big barn at the back, with a loft always

filled with sweet-smelling hay. Here in the evenings the two cows were milked and the mare was stabled for the night. Beyond the barn was the poultry yard, with the pigpens near at hand.

Stephen watched a grunting sow with her litter of clean squealing pigs. He thought what a pity it was that those round, pink, little ones would grow up to be just as fat and stupid and untidy as their mother. When he spoke this thought to Uncle Struthers, the old man laughed merrily.

"She's not much to look at," he agreed, "but she sure will make good lard and bacon. You can't always judge by the looks, Steve. I reckon 'handsome is as handsome does'!"

There were chickens and geese in the poultry yard. The turkeys foraged for themselves in a field some distance off and roosted in the trees at night.

"How do you keep them from flying away from your farm?" asked Stephen.

"Easy. Every evening I take some corn to the south pasture. They get to knowing about that good corn; so they always stay close to where it comes from. Kind of like people in that respect."

Stephen visited the dogs next. There were ten of them, and at sight of Stephen and Uncle Struthers they began to whine and bay, jumping and struggling to get out of their kennel yard.

"A little later we can go hunting," said Uncle Struthers. "About September would be a good time to get us a 'possum. We'll take the dogs and go across the woods. Pretty soon they'll pick up Mr. 'Possum's trail, and away they'll go, yelping and running like mad. First off, Mr. 'Possum will keep to cover, but before long he'll come out into the open and make a break for it. Then he'll see he can't make it; so up he'll go into the nearest tree. The hounds will sit around the base of the tree, their pink tongues hanging out a mile. They'll wait until we come. Then you'll shin up that tree where Mr. 'Possum is sitting out on a limb, playing dead. You'll shake him off for me to catch, and we'll take him home in a poke."

On the way back to the house Stephen chattered like a magpie about the promised hunt and other good times coming.

"We'll go coon-hunting, too, by the light of the moon," declared Uncle Struthers.

At the house, they found Mrs. Foster rummaging in cupboards for dishes. She had a chicken already tender in the pot, and biscuits ready for the oven of the old iron and brick cook-stove.

"Here," said Uncle Struthers to Stephen. "Take this pail and go down across the creek. You'll find plenty of blackberries along the fence. We can have them for dinner with cream and honey. Run, now, and don't keep us waiting."

Stephen was out of the house and down the hill like a rabbit. He knew where to find the mossy stepping-stones on which to cross the creek. Beyond the willows and the ferns was a sunny meadow enclosed with a gray rail fence. Around, over, and under the rails were thorny blackberry bushes, loaded with red and black fruit.

Stephen set to work, picking the luscious soft black fruit only; for he knew that the red fruit was unripe. Thorns scratched him, but a blackberry picker learns to think nothing of scratches. In a very short time his pail was full, and his mouth purple from the fruit he had eaten.

On his way back to the farmhouse, he stopped to pick some violets for his mother. They grew under the damp leaf-mold in places which caught only the morning sun. There were purple ones and white ones. Stephen was always to remember the sweet fragrance of these violets at Uncle Struthers', the field lilies that bloomed earlier, and the wild roses that sought out unsightly corners to cover with red and gold beauty.

Perhaps it was of those pleasant scenes of his childhood that Stephen Foster was thinking when he wrote his song *The Merry, Merry Month of May*.

THE MERRY, MERRY MONTH OF MAY

We roamed the fields and riv--er sides, When

we were young and gay; We chased the bees and

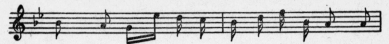

pluck'd the flowers, In the mer-ry, mer-ry month of

May. Oh, yes, with ev - er chang - ing sports, We

whiled the hours a - way; The

skies were bright, Our hearts were light, In the

mer - ry, mer - ry month of May.

Second Verse

Our voices echoed through the glen,
    With blithe and joyful ring;
We built our huts of mossy stones,
    And we dabbled in the hillside spring.

Third Verse

We joyed to meet and griev'd to part,
    We sigh'd when night came on;
We went to rest with longing heart,
    For the coming of the bright-day dawn.

Stephen returned with his berries to find a table set

for three in the kitchen. There were chicken and dumplings, biscuits and fried corncakes, onions from the garden, honey from the hives. There was a large pitcher of yellow cream, and a mound of sweet butter. Uncle Struthers washed the berries and put them in bowls. Mrs. Foster and Uncle Struthers chatted away, telling each other all the family gossip they knew. Stephen just ate.

After dinner, Mrs. Foster lay down to rest, and Stephen went with Uncle Struthers to mend fences at the far side of the farm. They walked past the beehives and the springhouse, and crossed a grove of hickory-nut trees and beeches.

In the evening, Stephen sat beside Uncle Struthers on the front stoop, watching the sun set. A few mosquitoes buzzed around, but Stephen scarcely noticed them because Uncle Struthers was telling him about the early days in Ohio. The old man had led an adventurous life, and he could tell about it in a storybook way.

He told Stephen how he and his wife, with several other families, had left their eastern home for the West:

"When we first came to the banks of the Ohio, we reckoned the worst part of our trip was over. Crossing the mountain passes of the Alleghenies with all our belongings had been the hardest part. We built flatboats to take us down the river. It took us weeks to build the boats—we had to cut down the trees and make planks from them with our axes. There weren't any sawmills in the wilderness in those days!

"Well, we loaded our household goods on these boats, and set off down the river. The boats weren't much more 'n rafts with small shelters on them. We steered with long oars and poles."

"That must have been fun," said Stephen, who loved the sights and sounds along the rivers.

"Not as easy as it sounds, I can tell you. You see, none of us knew the ways of the river. There were dangerous snags and sand bars that we had to steer clear of. Sometimes we had to fight our way out of a bad spot, using the poles till the muscles of our backs and arms seemed fair ready to burst.

"At night it was too dangerous to try to go on; so we'd tie up to some tree along the bank—and then be scared to death for fear some raiding party of Indians would come along. Chief Tecumseh was stirring up trouble in the North, and all the tribes were suspicious and sullen. Don't know as I blame them much, either, with hundreds of settlers coming in and turning their hunting grounds into fenced farms.

"But we didn't meet any Indians. We had a mighty nice trip down the river. By day some of us men would walk ashore and look for game to shoot. So we managed to have a little better food than just salt pork and bread. It was a long time, though, before we tasted food like the chicken and biscuits and fruit you had tonight. At first we had no chickens, and of course it took years to grow apple and peach and pear trees. Till our orchards were big enough to bear fruit, all we had was the wild berries and plums—and those only in summer, of course. We had to wait many months for our first crop of corn and potatoes, and longer than that to get seed for garden vegetables from 'the States.'

"What furniture we had was made by hand—with ax and pocket knife, adze and plane. Spinning-wheels were the only pieces of furniture that we brought along on the trip over the mountains, and I must say they gave a nice homey look to our bare cabins—for they *were* bare, just peeled logs and dirt floors till we had time to make tables and chairs and chests of drawers."

"How did you cook?" inquired Stephen. "Did you make stoves, too?"

"No." Uncle Struthers laughed. "We didn't make any stoves, as I remember! Meals were cooked in iron pots, spiders, and Dutch ovens set in the fireplace, where the fire was never allowed to go out. But don't you believe for a moment that we didn't have good eating, for we did. I guess there was never anything like those Indian puddings and roasted potatoes and turkeys barbecued on a turning spit. Of course, hunger is the best sauce, and it seemed like we were always hungry. Work made us that way. The men worked outdoors, building fences and felling trees to make room for gardens. The women made bedding, spun yarn from the wool and flax they had brought with them, and cut and sewed clothing for the men and children. The boys split rails for fences and cut wood for the fires, and the girls carried water and helped their mothers with the younger children."

"Did you work *all* the time?" Stephen, who liked play better than work, sounded disapproving.

99

"Oh, no," laughed Uncle Struthers. "We had fun, too. In the fall there were quilting parties. The women from all the cabins round about assembled at one place and made bedding for the cold winter months. They had saved every scrap of cloth left over from dresses and shirts. They pieced these together into tops for patchwork quilts. They made feather beds, too, with the feathers carefully saved from the poultry killed during the past months. In the evening the men joined them, even helping them with the sewing. There would be all kinds of jokes at their clumsy handling of the needle, and then there would be dinner and perhaps some music and dancing before we all went home through the gloomy forests.

"We had house-raisings, too. Know what a house-raising is, Steve?—When all the neighbors got together to help a newcomer build his log cabin? People knew how to work together in those days. They knew that many hands make light work, and that cheerfulness and friendship make the task lighter still. There was sure to be dancing to the music of the fiddles when the work was done, and a feast on plank tables set on the fresh-cut stumps.

"In the fall we gathered hickory nuts. We picked the wild persimmons with the first frost on them, and gathered the bark of the witch-hazel to be used as medicine. In the spring we boiled down the sap from the maple trees, and made golden syrup and sugar. That was work, but we made play of it, too."

100

Uncle Struthers

"Did you ever have fights with the Indians?" Stephen's drowsy voice told how sleepy he was, but he was careful to make his eyes look wide awake so that the tales of long ago would not come to an end.

"Too many," said Uncle Struthers. "Too many for comfort! Whenever we heard there was unrest among the tribes, we got scared, I can tell you. Sometimes a scout would come to our settlement in the dead of night to warn us of bad Indians coming our way. The minute that happened, all of us got together in the largest cabin—women and children and all. We carried water and food inside to last us for a long time, and stood ready with our rifles in case we were attacked.

"Once," went on Uncle Struthers with a twinkle in his eye, "we had some Indian trouble when there wasn't an Indian within twenty miles of us. Yes, sir, we had an Injun fight without any Injuns!"

"Now you're fooling," Stephen said, disappointed.

"No, young Stevie, I'm not fooling. This is the way it was: We had left the settlement, about fifteen of us men, to hunt. At intervals we went out in large parties this way to get a supply of venison to jerk for winter.

"We had heard that the Indian tribes were having a powwow and might go on the warpath at any time; so we took certain precautions. Four of our number, the best scouts of the settlement, were told off to travel to either side and before and behind the main party so as to sniff out danger. They traveled just out of sight, but were never very far from us.

101

"Well, pretty soon—after two or three weeks—we'd got used to our scouts being 'invisible,' and had almost forgotten the Indian scare. And then, all of a sudden, what was our surprise one morning to see the advance scout trot down the trail to meet us with the word that Indians were ahead!

"Each man immediately checked his rifle, making sure it was loaded and that his powder horn and shot were handy. Then we took to the cover of the big trees, slipping forward Indian fashion, keeping an eye on our scout, and darting swiftly and as noiselessly as possible from cover to cover.

"I watched every movement of our scout. I saw him freeze into sudden immobility against the trunk of a huge sycamore. He had sighted an enemy. I followed the line of his rifle barrel with my eye. Not ten paces in front of him was another huge tree; at one side of it a stray sunbeam glinted on a rifle barrel. All the Indians in our section of the country had rifles in those days.

"Well, I tell you, what followed looked mighty like a game. Our man was very careful not to show himself, but at the same time he kept trying, by sudden movements of his rifle, to decoy the enemy into the open. But the enemy was as wise as a fox; only the tip of his rifle barrel could be seen, and an occasional leather fringe—nothing to be shot at. Patiently the scout waited. His opponent was *just* as patient.

"Then — when we least expected it — the enemy streaked across the clearing. Moccasined feet took him

102

swiftly to the cover of an oak to the right of our scout. Quick as lightning the woodsman changed his position. The enemy's jacket flashed briefly into view. Long enough for our man. *Bang! Bang!* The foe had drawn our scout's fire, but had not been hit.

"While the scout reloaded with powder and shot, another of our men took up the stalking chase. Craftily he exposed for one instant his stout right arm. *Bang! Bang!* The enemy's fire had been drawn at last. We closed in, giving him no chance to reload.

" 'Come out of it, you skulking redskin!' shouted one of our party.

"What was our amazement to hear a white man answer in drawling, disgusted tones: 'Redskin nuthin'! Thought that was what *you* was.' And emerging from the cover of the oak came one of our own scouts!

"Well, the whole thing was so funny that we laughed till we frightened all the little wood creatures into bushes and burrows. It seems that the right-hand scout, traveling faster than he realized, had advanced beyond the main party. Pausing to get his bearings, he had been surprised by the head scout. Each had but a fleeting glimpse of the other. In the dim half-light of the forest they had mistaken each other for Indians. Naturally, they didn't stop for introductions—they just leaped for the nearest tree, and started three hours of the prettiest stalking I ever saw."

Stephen laughed gleefully at this story of an "Injun

103

fight without Injuns," then asked, "Would you have to fight redskins if you went hunting now?"

"Hardly," said Uncle Struthers. "We're pretty safe and humdrum around here now. The Government has taken most of the Ohio and Mississippi tribes north of us into the Indiana country, as they call it—rounded 'em up and made 'em stay there. Today, you can go clear to the Gulf, by land or by river, and never see an Indian—or maybe just one or two traveling on business for the tribes.

"In those days, though, you couldn't go many miles without running into a party of them. You were lucky if it was a hunting party and not a scalping expedition.

"Even boys of your age, Stevie, learned to carry rifles wherever they went. Puts me in mind of the time three boys not a day older than you were carried off by a band of Shawnees."

"Tell me about it!" demanded Stephen eagerly.

"Well," began Uncle Struthers, "those boys had gone across the river to hunt. They weren't supposed to go so far away from the clearing where the cabins were, but I guess you know how it is—boys don't always mind the way they should. First thing they knew, a bunch of naked savages had them surrounded. The Indians just stood about, grinning at them, showing no intention of harming the youngsters; but when one of the boys raised his rifle to fire an alarm for the settlement across the river, he got a sound cuff for his trouble. The Indians motioned the boys to go ahead of them through the forest, but didn't take away their arms. A Shawnee warrior considered it a disgrace to be disarmed by an enemy, and these Indians were treating the boys the same as they would have expected to be treated, themselves, if they had been captured.

"The boys pretended that they liked the idea of going with the Indians. They had heard that the redskins had strange notions about harming children, and often preferred to adopt them into the tribe. They did not let the warriors see that they were afraid, though they were shaking in their boots, you can be sure. They went quietly with their captors to the tribal tents, three long marches away.

"For several months the boys lived peacefully with the Indians, who were kind to them but kept watch for any sign that the boys planned escape. The boys, homesick for their parents and their homes, planned nothing else. Finally, one night, their chance came. Remember, they were more than a hundred miles from their Ohio home, but that thought did not stop them from slipping into the dark forest. Rifles in hand, they sneaked stealthily past the watchfires of the Indians, and by daybreak they were many miles on their way.

"They hunted game to feed themselves. They traveled night and day. They didn't dare to rest a moment, for they knew that the best trackers of the tribe would be after them, and that recapture would mean a horrible death by torture. They used all the forest lore they had in order to throw the pursuers off the scent. They walked down the beds of streams so as to cover their trail. They

105

walked on the rocky places of open ground so as to leave no footprints. In the forests, they walked on pine needles, which tell no tales. They got their direction by observing the position of the sun and the stars.

"Staggering, limping, pausing to lift one who fell exhausted on the trail, helping him along till he found the courage to go on his own strength again, eating raw the game they killed for fear of attracting notice with a fire, they covered the weary miles. Ragged and near dead from hardship, they stumbled into the settlement early one morning. We had long since given them up for lost; so you can imagine what rejoicing there was, and how their mothers laughed and cried at the same time to see their boys again. We put them to bed, and let them sleep all day, but that night we had a feast in their honor. While we ate pumpkin and corncakes and wild turkey, they told us their story over and over again, until they fell asleep. . . . And that's just what you're doing—" Uncle Struthers broke off. "Here! Off to bed with you, before I have to carry you, my fine young brave!"

So Stephen told Uncle Struthers and his mother goodnight, and his mother tucked him into the "shook" bed in the lean-to behind the kitchen. With his head full of the tales of long ago, Stephen closed his eyes to sleep peacefully until the crowing of the roosters should wake him the next morning.

CHAPTER NINE

GOING AWAY TO SCHOOL

STEPHEN'S FATHER AND MOTHER were talking late before the fire one cold night in January. They were worrying about Stephen—a big boy of thirteen and a half now that the year 1840 had come, but he had not yet decided what work he would follow for the rest of his life. At that time boys went to work when they were very young, or at least began early to prepare themselves for some chosen profession. Already the other Foster boys had been working for several years. Stephen alone remained at home—which now was Youngstown, Ohio— showing no desire to prepare himself to make a living.

"It is partly my fault, William," said Mrs. Foster. "I could not bear to force the boy to go to school when he hated it so much. He is a good, sweet boy. He studies faithfully at home and fools about none at all. Still, I think it would be good for him to go regularly to school. He has grown moody and shy."

"He spends too much time with his music, Mother!" declared Mr. Foster sternly. "No good will come of it. Music is not a gentleman's profession. It leads people into idle ways at the best, and at the worst, well—"

"I know. As a profession, it is out of the question for

107

Stevie, of course. But I have seen no harm in letting him study it as a pastime. Music, after all, is a very great art."

"It is not the music itself I object to," argued Stephen's father. "Music in the home is a splendid thing. I like to draw a few notes on the violin myself. But to make a profession of it! To play the steam calliope on a show-boat! To run with song-writing minstrels!"

"But, Pa, dear, Stevie *might* become a great concert artist. That child, Jenny Lind, that we have read about, for instance—"

"No money in it," snorted Mr. Foster. "For a few, yes. For the usual run of the mill, no."

"Uncle Struthers always said that Stephen would grow up to be a great man," said Mrs. Foster wistfully.

"Let him be great, then. A great engineer. A great soldier. A great sailor. A great steamboat pilot. Anything but a great musician."

"I suppose you are right," sighed Mrs. Foster. "I wish we could be sure what is best to do."

Brother William came into the room at that moment. He was on one of his rare visits to Youngstown, and would leave shortly for Towanda. With Towanda as headquarters, he would begin his new work as principal engineer of canals and railroads in eastern Pennsylvania. His level eyes and firm jaw made it clear that he was a man of business, a practical man, a man who would get things done.

"I couldn't help overhearing some of your conversation about Steve," he said. "And I have a suggestion. Why not

let me look after him for a while? Let him go with me
to Towanda. I will pay his way in the Athens Academy.
It is a fine old school, close enough to Towanda for me
to keep in touch with him while he is there."

"You always come to the rescue of the Foster family,"
Mr. Foster sighed. "I am afraid we ask too much of you."

"Nonsense!" Brother William laughed. "Who was it
that came to my rescue when I was a homeless little boy,
with no one to look after me? Besides, I am making good
money now, and I can afford to be generous."

"It might be a very good thing for Stephen," Mrs.
Foster said thoughtfully. "He needs a change of scene.
And of course we all know how much he loves you,
William."

Mr. Foster nodded his head. "It may be the means of
getting him to forget his songs and his flute. If you are
really willing, William, I shall be, too."

"I'll tell Steve," said William, "the minute he comes
in."

Stephen came home, his clothes powdered with snow.
His olive cheeks glowed red from cold and exercise. He
had been walking by himself in the white woods.

"How would you like to go away from home for a
while, Steve? To school?" Brother William put an affectionate arm around Stephen's shoulders.

Stephen looked suddenly troubled. "Where do you
want me to go?" he asked in a low voice.

"With me. To Towanda. Then to Athens, where you
could attend Athens Academy. It is a beautiful school.

You would love it. The two-story building is long, with tall chimneys at each end. Classrooms are on the ground floor. The upper rooms have desks and tables for study hours. The school overlooks two rivers at Tioga Point— the Susquehanna and the Chemung. There would be skating in winter, and boating in summer, and fishing. All kinds of sports with boys of your own age. What do you say, Stephen?"

Stephen had been looking from one face to the other. He did not want to go away from Youngstown. All his life he loved his home so much that he could never be happy for very long away from it. Home meant mother and father. Where they were Stephen longed to be. But he saw that both his father and mother wanted him to agree to William's plan. With a heavy heart he did agree, and he tried to smile, because it was his nature not to hurt others or to disappoint them.

The trip to Towanda was an adventure. Stephen was happier about going away to school when Brother William told him that they would make the entire journey by sleigh. The distance to be covered was more than four hundred miles, and it would take them many days.

Early one January morning in 1840 they were ready to go. Mrs. Foster bundled Stephen into the seat beside William with heavy blankets and a buffalo robe on top of all. She had placed two warm bricks in the bottom of the sleigh to keep the frost from Stephen's and William's feet.

110

Going Away to School

The countryside was white with snow, and the roads were packed and frozen. Trees lay half-buried in their frozen drifts. Stephen's breath rose like the smoke from the chimneys of the cottages.

His mother kissed him and cried a little and begged William to be careful in driving the two spirited horses hitched to the cutter. His father said, "Mit and Dunning are expecting you in Pittsburgh. They have a present or two for you, Stephen."

With shouted good-byes, they were off. The cutter sped over the hard roads. The horses trotted briskly, as if they, too, enjoyed the idea of a long trip in the sparkling cold. Now and again clumps of ice from their hooves struck the high dashboard, and a few smaller particles stung Stephen's face.

William was a well-known and very popular man. All along the way he and Stephen stopped at homes and inns where people welcomed them with friendship and warm meals. At night when Stephen was tired from traveling, and was cold and hungry besides, it was good to pull up before a cheery inn, where a fire blazed on the wide hearth. Ham and cornbread had never before tasted so good to Stephen, and a feather bed had never seemed so comfortable.

They rose with the sun every morning. After a breakfast of fried mush and molasses, sausage, and milk they were ready for the road again.

After a visit with Mit and Dunning in Pittsburgh, they

111

set out for Harrisburg. In that city Brother William took Stephen to the building occupied by the State Legislature, where he saw how members of the House of Representatives voted on new laws for Pennsylvania. The two travelers called on the Governor, and in the evening went to a concert. Then they were on their way again, and on January 27, Stephen was in school.

Stephen boarded with a Mr. Herrick and his family. He was not very happy in this household, as a letter he wrote to Brother William shows:

Dear Brother: *

As Mr. Mitchell is going to start for Towanda today, I thougt I would write you a line concerning my studies as he says you will not be here for more than a week.

My Philosophy Grammar & Arithmetic not being enough to keep me going I would ask your permision to Study either Latin or Bookkeeping.

I have no place to study in the evenings as the little ones at Mr. Herricks keep such a crying and talking that it's imposible to read. There is a good fire place in my room and if you will just say the word I will have a fire in it at nights and learn something. When you come dont forget my waistcoat at the tailors. there are several little articles which I need though I have no room to mention them. I must stop writing as I am very cold.

Your affectionate Brother
STEPHEN.

Stephen was so unhappy at Athens that William presently allowed him to come to Towanda, where he at-

---

* The form of this letter and the following is that of the originals.

tended the Towanda Academy. Stephen was almost content at Towanda. When he learned that William considered sending him back to Athens he wrote a pleading letter to his brother, who was busy surveying a route for canals and railroads.

My Dear Brother.

As you wish to have me go to Athens for fear I will not learn enough in this place, I will tell you what my ideas were on the subject.

Mr. Vosberry is a very good mathematition, and as he has quit keeping school, he is going to ocupy a private room in the house of Mr. Elwell.

Mr. Kettle will be here tomorrow and will stop at Bartlett & Fords. he will have a room there but will not be in it in the day-time as his paint room will be at another house. Mr. Ford says he will board me and give me as good a room as I wish for $2.00 per week.

If you will let me board here (while you stay) and room with Kettle I will promise not to be seen out of doors betwen the hours of nine & twelve A.M. and one & four P.M. Which hours I will attribute to study, such as you please to put me into. I will also promise not to pay any attention to my music untill after eight Oclock in the evening after which time Mr. Kettle will probably be in the room as he cannot paint after dark. I dont se how I could have a better chance for study. & the above price is as cheap as I could live in Athens that lonesome place—I can go over to recite in the forenoon at about 10 oclock and in the afternoon at 4—do please consent.

Your affectionate & grateful brother

STEPHEN

Please pay Mr. D. Mitchell $3.00 which I borowed from him to pay for pumps, subscription &c for the exhibition. I allso owe Mr. Vandercook a very small amount.

Dont pay Mr. Herrick for fire in my room as I have not had any since you payed him last.

In that letter written to Brother William, Stephen left a remarkable picture of himself. He did not realize how much he was telling. It is fairly certain that businesslike William did not read all that was between the lines.

The letter was written by a shy, sensitive boy, craving the warmth of friendship. He must have been very lonesome in Athens. When he speaks of "Athens that lonesome place" it is like a cry of pain. He felt neglected by Mr. Herrick, and was made more uncomfortable by the older man's chilly manner than he was by the iciness of his fireless bedroom.

Stephen probably brushed the tears from his eyes as he wrote that letter, hurriedly so that no one would see his weakness. He was begging to be left in a happier place, and in return he was prepared to make a great sacrifice. "I will promise not to pay any attention to my music. . . ." Brother William could not have known how the boy's hand faltered as he wrote those words.

Brother William may not have understood Stephen's reasons, but he had a kind heart and he wanted his young brother to be happy. He allowed Stephen to remain in Towanda.

Stephen tried hard to live up to his promises. His

beloved flute was brought out only in leisure hours. He struggled with the dry knowledge that was supposed to fit him for a place in life. He wanted to live up to the high hopes his mother and father had. He wanted to make Uncle Struthers proud. And because so many of the persons who advised him were mistaken, Stephen was mistaken, too: he neglected his music.

With melodies singing in his head, he did little or nothing to master the forms and rules necessary for a composer to know. All his life he was to suffer from this neglect. Though he wrote some of the finest melodies ever set down, he never knew how to make other than the simplest accompaniments for them. With adequate training he might have written symphonies and operas. Limited as he was, he wrote only simple songs. Sometimes he even made mistakes in setting down notes, and musicians laughed at him. In spite of all these handicaps, however, his genius was to carry him forward until he became America's best-loved composer.

Stephen was making so little progress in his school work that by the summer of 1841 it was decided that he should return home. But before he left, he composed his first piece of music—the urge to create had been too much for his resolve to forget his chief enthusiasm. This was the *Tioga Waltz* for flutes, and at the Commencement exercises of the Athens Academy on April 1, 1841, it was performed by Stephen and three classmates. Here is the first part of it:

THE TIOGA WALTZ

Stephen Foster, whether he knew it or not, had chosen his life work when he wrote that simple melody.

CHAPTER TEN

"DREAMING THE HAPPY HOURS AWAY"

FOR THE NEXT five years, Stephen was living where he wanted to live: at home with his parents, who had returned to Pittsburgh while he was at school. Mr. Foster was awaiting an expected appointment to a position in the Treasury Department at Washington, D. C. Mit, employed as clerk and messenger by the owner of a Pittsburgh cotton mill, Mr. McCormick, was quite content with a hundred dollars a year in wages, in addition to his board and room plus a pony furnished him for trips about the town. As for Henry, he was learning to be a surveyor with Brother William.

When Stephen joined the Pittsburgh household in May, 1841, the family councils began again. What should be done with this gentle-mannered boy who tried with all his might to do as his parents wished and yet could not make a success of his schooling?

It was decided at last to send him to Canonsburg, to the school that his father had attended when it was known as Log College. The name had been changed to Jefferson College, in honor of the third president of the United States.

With the best intentions Stephen went to Canonsburg, which was only eighteen miles from his home. As soon as he was enrolled in the school he wrote to William:

My Dear Brother,

I arrived here on last Tuesday, and found among the quantity of Students of this institution, several of my old acquaintances.

This is a very pretty situation where I board as it is on an elivation of about four hundred feet. We have about two hundred and thirty students here at the present time, and a library of about 1500 volumes.

Pa left this [place] on Wednesday last and is now at Warren I believe.

The tuition instead of being $5.00 amounts to $12.50 and boarding $2.00 per week.

Pa paid my tuition bill in advance, as is customary at this place. Their is several other bills which I have not paid as I have not the means. Such as 2 or $3.00 for joining one of the literary societies, as all of the studens belong to them I was requested to joiin one and put it of for a couple of weeks, for as Pa has not much more than the means of geting along I thought I would write you this letter that you might considder over the matter. I will also have to pay boarding bill at the end of every month which will amount to $8.50 that is at the end of four weeks and a half which generally makes a month, and if you see fit to send me a little of the bino. once in a while I will insure you their is no inducements here to make me spend any money unnecesarily. I will allso have to pay about $1.25 per week for washing as I have to keep myself very clean here.

I would inform you in the meantime I need another summer coat or two and especially for Sunday.

"Dreaming the Happy Hours Away"

The Ohio river is very low and falling gradually. The boats have ceased runing.

As I have made out a mideling long letter and am clear out of informations (news) I would only say, wishing you a safe journey home and through life, and that I may some day be fit to render thanks to you for your unceasing kindness to me. I remain your ever grateful and affectionate brother

Stephen

William probably shook his head when he saw Stephen's poor spelling and smiled at his cautious mention of money matters. However, he must have had little time to "considder over the matter"; for Stephen did not remain at Canonsburg.

Stephen could not enter into the life of the new school. He was homesick, though he was careful not to say so. After all, he was a big boy, almost a man. The other students and even his family would have laughed at him and called him a baby. Perhaps that is what he was.

His father worried because Stephen was not preparing to make his way in the world. His mother worried because Stephen was unhappy and homesick. No one seemed to worry about the most important fact of all— that Stephen was running away from difficulties instead of meeting and overcoming them. All his life Stephen suffered because he had not learned to face his troubles.

Mr. Foster wrote Brother William, telling of Stephen's discontent:

Stephen will not stay at Cannonsburg—he says he has lost conseat of himself because he was once in his life a great fool,

119

and that was when he did not go back with brother William.
He begs me to ask you to say that he must board with Ma
and go to day skool . . .

Mrs. Foster wrote:

Indeed, if I am in Allegheny Town I shall be almost too
lonely without one child with me, for if I should be ill, I would
be in a bad way.

Stephen sent a letter full of excuses and apologies:

My Dear Brother,

I suppose you are surprised and probably displeased at me
for not being more punctual in writing to you every fortnight,
as you wished to have me do. I will therefore proceed to make
my best excuses.

When I wrote to you from Canonsburg I did not tell you
whether I liked the place or not (if I remember aright) but
now I will take the liberty of telling you that I became more
disgusted with the place as long as I stayed in it. It is not a
good time to begin college in the middle of the Session as I
could not get into any class for three or four days after I went
there, and when I did get started into a recitation it was in
irregular hours.

If I had went as a regular student I might have been
examined and got along very easily, but going as I did just to
stay a session or two, I suppose they did not care much
whether I was attended to or not. Besides, when I had been
there but five days I took sick (from a disiness in my head
occasioned by an overflow of the blood) and was confined to
bed for two days.

Stephen stayed exactly seven days in Canonsburg!
In August the family moved into a house belonging to

Brother William. This house was located on a pleasant spot facing the East Common in Allegheny City. Not far off was the Allegheny River, with Pittsburgh on the opposite bank.

Stephen settled into the quiet life of Allegheny with contentment. He spent long hours walking along the river, enjoying the still summer days. The bells of the new church on the East Common rang out pleasantly on Sunday mornings, and Stephen went with his mother to attend the services. On week-days he sometimes hitched the sorrel mare to the old box buggy and drove with his mother into Pittsburgh, where he lingered in a music shop while she did her buying and visiting.

At night he lighted the lamp in his room and read. He was fond of the works of Edgar Allan Poe, whose somber stories and poems held a great fascination for him.

Stephen took up his studies in a school near his home. His father wrote to William:

I regret extremely that Stephen has not been able to appreciate properly your generous exertions in his behalf, by availing himself of the advantage of a college education, which will cause him much regret before he arrives at my age; and he will no doubt express those regrets in much sorrow to you. . . .

He is at school, now, with Mr. Moody, a first rate teacher of mathematics in Pittsbg. and it is a source of much comfort to your mother and myself, that he does not appear to have any evil propensities to indulge; he seeks no associates; and his leisure hours are all devoted to musick, for which he possesses a strange talent.

121

By the end of November, Mr. Foster was in Washington, D. C., ready to assume the duties of his position in the Treasury Department. Mrs. Foster and her boys remained in Allegheny City, living quietly and contentedly among the old friends and neighbors.

Every day Stephen walked faithfully into Pittsburgh, where he studied mathematics with Mr. Moody. The noise of the rivers rose on frosty mornings as of old. The days grew cool, then cold, and eventually there was an end of the river traffic for a while. The Ohio was icebound.

During the winter Stephen became acquainted with Captain Jean Herbst, a Belgian who taught French and German. Stephen was permitted to take lessons from him and on winter evenings before the fire in Captain Herbst's study, the two talked together.

The teacher spoke sometimes in French, sometimes in German. It was not long before Stephen understood and spoke these languages fairly well; for he learned easily what he wanted to learn.

Jean Herbst sat before his coal fire and spoke longingly of his boyhood home in Belgium. There was a catch in his voice when he told his pupil about Liége and the winding River Meuse. Stephen understood how Captain Herbst felt, for the homesick days at Athens and Canonsburg were fresh in his mind.

Captain Herbst was a man of great book-learning. He was fond of telling Stephen about the famous French authors of the century just past. There was first of all Voltaire, clever and witty and untiring in his efforts to aid the oppressed people of France and of the world. Then there was Jean-Jacques Rousseau, whose ideas about human rights and freedom had been borrowed by the makers of our Declaration of Independence.

Jean Herbst talked of Goethe, the greatest poet of the German people, as if he had been an old friend, telling of the German poet's meetings with Mozart and Beethoven, those Titans of the musical world. Stephen heard, too, of the Brothers Grimm, the two learned Germans who went about listening to the folk-tales of their countrymen and wrote them down for the first time. Like the music of Lieve's people, those tales were made up by the humble folk, who remembered the best stories and passed them on from generation to generation. There were the stories about the witch and the soldier, and the dog with eyes as big as mill-wheels; about the donkey, the dog, the cat, and the cock who wanted to become musicians in Bremen Town; about Hänsel and Gretel; and about Snow White and the Seven Dwarfs.

Stephen's interest in German and in music led him into friendship with Henry Kleber, a musician and teacher who had come to America from Darmstadt, Germany. Mr. Kleber and his brother had a music store in Pittsburgh. In that store Stephen was always welcome. The Klebers allowed him to play one of their pianos, since the young musician had none at home. Brother William's piano, which had been a gift for Charlotte, had

123

long ago been sold and the money used to pay bills during a lean year in the Foster household.

The Klebers were very fond of the quiet boy with the dark, dreaming eyes. They encouraged his dreams. They told him stories of their own youth. For him they sang German folk-songs, and played the zither, which is the German folk instrument.

Stephen liked to hear their tales about the little town of Darmstadt. Henry Kleber explained that Darmstadt was in Hesse, the small German duchy from which many soldiers had been recruited by the British to fight against the Colonial army of George Washington. These recruits were the Hessian mercenaries, sold into military service much as slaves are sold. Their German lord received a certain amount of money for every man he sold into service, and an additional sum if the man was killed. Many of the Hessians, said the Klebers, deserted the British army and settled down in America to become good citizens of the United States.

The Klebers were quick to notice Stephen's musical ability. When he had a moment to spare, Henry Kleber showed Stephen what he knew about music. He helped the boy with his practising, and explained the simpler rules of composition.

In the pleasant little back room with its clutter of books and music sheets and clocks and pipes and a canary in a willow cage, Stephen made himself at home. It was not long before he was improvising music. Then it was but a step to putting down these improvised melodies on

paper. Henry Kleber looked them over and made corrections. Thus it was that the boy developed his "strange talent for music."

It was Henry Kleber who gave Stephen the books and music necessary for study. He told him about the great Mozart, who at the age of four had composed simple minuets, and had written an opera before he was twelve. Of course, Mr. Kleber pointed out, Mozart had a father who was a musician and composer, and he had taught his son early how to set down on paper the melodies that sang in the child's head. Henry Kleber also told Stephen about the giant among composers—Beethoven.

"The works of these men you must study," said Mr. Kleber, lending Stephen home-made folios of sonatas and concertos and symphonies. "And this is another composer you must know," he added, giving Stephen a few of Franz Schubert's songs.

Every evening Stephen's lamp burned late in his little room under the eaves. Mozart and Beethoven were too difficult for him to master. He needed more knowledge than he had or could get alone. He needed a teacher very badly—a teacher with a more substantial background in music than the amiable but limited Mr. Kleber.

The songs of Schubert were different. Stephen understood them. They were simple but beautiful expressions of the spirit of the German and Austrian people, compositions that have since been called *lieder*—the German word for "songs"—and which in many ways closely resemble real "folk-songs." Perhaps this is why they appealed to Stephen. The musical urge within him was closely akin to the spirit that creates folk music, and in later years, he was often called the American Schubert.

Mrs. Foster's sympathetic heart yearned over Stephen and his love for music. Somehow she managed to get a piano for him. Doubting whether she was doing the wise thing to encourage his talent, she was nevertheless confirmed in her decision when she saw her son's face light up with joy at the sight of the precious new possession.

In the book that Mit wrote about his famous brother is a picture of the young man working at his music:

He would sit at home in the evening at the piano and improvise by the hour beautiful strains and harmonies which he did not preserve, but let them float away like fragrant flowers cast upon the flowing water. Occasionally he would vary his occupation by singing in plaintive tones one of his own or other favorite songs. Of the latter class he much admired the "May Queen" of Tennyson, and the music as composed by Mr. Dempster. His rendering of the verse "Tonight I saw the sun set, he set and left behind," etc., was truly pathetic. At times tears could be seen on his cheeks as he sang this song, so sensitive was his nature to the influence of true poetry combined with music. I usually sat near him on these occasions and listened quietly with profound delight. Sometimes he would whirl round on the piano stool and converse a few moments with me, then resume his improvisations and his singing.

While Stephen studied music, and dreamed his pleasant dreams through the short winter days, the uncertain days of spring, and the long lazy days of summer, the

126

world moved on. Events did not touch Stephen, however. It was almost as if he walked in his sleep.

The great Charles Dickens came to America. He became ill while he was in Pittsburgh and took treatment from Dr. McDowell, the father of the fair "Jeanie with the light brown hair."

Stephen and his father went to call on the author during his stay at the Monongahela House, an old-fashioned hotel with columns and balconies and draughty, high-ceilinged rooms. "Boz" was sick and cranky, though polite, and he was far too much annoyed at the general run of tobacco-chewing American men and boys to pay much attention to the shy, reserved lad who bowed politely to him and hoped he would be feeling better soon. Stephen Foster and Charles Dickens were like the barge and the steamer passing on the river: they came abreast of each other, shouted a friendly hello without paying much attention to each other, and passed by never to see each other again.

The years wore on. One fall edged into another winter, and the next spring slipped into summer. Stephen drifted like the clouds of summer, quietly and peacefully. His legs grew longer. His voice deepened. But life had not yet touched him.

There were various changes in the family. Mr. Foster returned from Washington and in December 1841 was elected Mayor of Allegheny. Henry took a position in the Land Office at Washington, and in February 1842 his mother went "over the mountains" to pay a visit to him and also to some Baltimore friends and relatives. In the spring Henrietta's husband died; and in the autumn Brother William married the lovely Elizabeth Burnett. Since 1840, Dunning had been a clerk on a steamboat, but by 1846 he was in business in Cincinnati.

Meanwhile Stephen remained at home, "dreaming the happy hours away." This was the phrase he later used in a beautiful love song that tells us better than words could do of the Stephen Foster to whom the quiet, peaceful things of life were always dear. It begins like this:

COME WHERE MY LOVE LIES DREAMING

128

"Dreaming the Happy Hours Away"

Come where my loves lies dream-ing, Yes, is sweet-ly.

dream - ing the hap -py hours a - way.

Come with a lute, come with a lay, My

own love is sweet-ly dream - ing, Her beau-ty

beam-ing; Come where my love lies dreaming, Yes, is

sweet-ly dream-ing the hap-py hours a - way.

129

CHAPTER ELEVEN

FRIENDS

THE HOUSE ON the East Common had neighbors. Across the way lived Andrew Robinson, friend of the Foster boys. Next door to the Fosters was the home of the Pentlands. A gate opened in the fence between the two houses. Through this gate young Susan, who was about five years younger than Stephen, would run over to visit him and to listen wide-eyed when he sang.

One day, when Stephen was sixteen, he sang a special song for the little girl with the laughing eyes. The words of this song were a poem written by George P. Morris. The same words had already been set to music by the English song-writer Joseph Philip Knight. Knight was a musician of great popularity, noted especially for his song *Rocked in the Cradle of the Deep*. Knight was a thoroughly trained musician, and the music he wrote for Morris' poem was the work of maturity and experience. Yet his music is almost forgotten today; whereas the simple melody that Stephen wrote when he was a boy lives on in the beautiful serenade *Open Thy Lattice, Love*. Here is the song he wrote and dedicated to little Susan:

130

OPEN THY LATTICE, LOVE

O - pen thy lat-tice, love, lis-ten to me! The cool bal-my breeze is a - broad on the sea! The moon, like a queen, roams her realms of blue, And the stars keep their vi-gils in hea-ven for you. Ere morn's gush-ing light tips the hills with its ray, A - way o'er the wa - ters a - way and a - way! Then o-pen thy lat-tice, love, lis-ten to me! While the moon's in the sky and the breeze on the sea!

131

There were other friends besides Andy and Susan. When Stephen strolled along the busy streets of Pittsburgh, Dr. McDowell's phaeton often passed him, and Jane and Agnes and Marion leaned over the side to call hello. They had to shout to make him hear; for Stephen went about lost to the world, holding the notebook which he always carried so that he could jot down the lyrics and melodies that came to him.

The young composer was only vaguely aware, as he walked through the streets, of the high-stepping horses, the ladies and girls mincing along in rustling silks and kid boots, the young dandies with collars carelessly open in imitation of the poet Byron. It was always so with Stephen. He enjoyed walking or driving in the city—yet he noticed little of what went on around him. He was always thinking of new songs. As they came to him, he jotted notes down instantly—in his notebook, on his cuff, even on his thumb-nail if there was no other surface on which to write. He scarcely heard the draymen yelling at the huge horses pulling loads of freight, or the factory whistles calling the workers to the foundries. In the midst of the increasing clamor of a growing industrial city, Stephen heard only the sounds of a peaceful countryside.

There was a group of young people who met together to play the piano and sing. These included "Ginny" and Annie Crosson, Annie and "Lib" Ogden, Julia Murray, Caroline Denny, J. Cust Blair, Mary Keller, and a club of young men who called themselves "The Knights of the S. T.," of which Mit and Stephen were members.

These friends went picnicking together along the rivers in spring. They went berrying in late summer, and took hay rides. At Christmas time they went skating and sledding on the frozen rivers. At Christmas, too, there was a round of holiday parties, when the boys kissed the girls under the mistletoe. Mit and Julia were teased for being sweethearts, and so were Steve and Mary. Sometimes they danced—the sedate quadrille or the gay polka. An evening never ended without the group gathering round a piano and singing.

Most of the songs they sang were those they had learned from the groups of traveling families of singers who stopped often in Pittsburgh. These were usually woefully sad ballads such as *Down in the Valley:*

> Down in the valley,
>   Valley so low—
> Hang your head over;
>   Hear the wind blow.
> Hear the wind blow, dear;
>   Hear the wind blow;
> Hang your head over,
>   And hear the wind blow.

They sang the old Scotch airs like *Auld Lang Syne* and sometimes an Irish song full of impudence and humor. Such a one was *Kitty of Coleraine.* This song told the story of pretty Kitty, who was so busy looking at the

133

handsome Barney McCleary that she tripped and fell and broke the pitcher she was carrying home from the fair of Coleraine. She began to weep, and—but let Barney tell the story from that point on:

> "I sat down beside her, and gently did chide her,
> That such a misfortune should give her such pain.
> A kiss then I gave her, and ere I did leave her,
> She vowed, for such pleasure, she'd break it again.
> 'Twas hay-making season, I can't tell the reason,
> Misfortunes will never come single, 'tis plain;
> For very soon after poor Kitty's disaster
> The divil a pitcher was whole in Coleraine."

And of course at Christmas time they sang carols. One of their favorites, when the candles had been lighted on the boughs of the Christmas tree, and the hot crabapples were hissing in the cider, was *The First Nowell:*

> "The first Nowell the angels did say
> Was to certain poor shepherds in fields as they lay,
> In fields as they lay keeping their sheep
> On a cold winter's night that was so deep.
> *Nowell, Nowell, Nowell, Nowell!*
> Born is the King of Israel!"

Stephen enjoyed such merry evenings with his friends, but he avoided the stiff, formal parties of Pittsburgh. Morrison's book tells how Stephen disliked people who invited him not for himself but for his ability to entertain the other guests with his music:

134

Friends

It was difficult to get him to go into society at all. He had a great aversion to its shams and glitter, and preferred the realities of his home and the quiet of his study. When he was eighteen years old, a lady who was an old friend of the family, gave a large party, and invited us all, and added, "Tell Stephen to bring his flute with him." That settled it so far as he was concerned. He would not go a step. He said, "tell Mrs. ——— I will send my flute if she desires it." This dislike to being classed as a mere performer characterized him during his whole life, though he was not at all unsocial and willingly sang or played for the enjoyment of himself or others, if the occasions were spontaneous and not set up. He, however, often sang in chorus with others, upon occasions of concerts for charitable purposes, in Pittsburgh."

Stephen's mother and father could not help worrying about their son. He spent much time wandering alone in the woods and along the rivers with his books and pencils. He learned to make watercolor sketches pale of tint and delicate of line. He studied mathematics less and less. He wrote poetry in a little book, and he wrote music.

For hours he would lie under the willows by the river, staring at the clouds piling up in the sky, letting the lint-covered seeds of the cottonwoods blow over his face. Idle, some folk called him, but he was not idle: he was thinking, and his thoughts were songs.

Mit was away from Pittsburgh much of the time, making long business trips to New Orleans, for he was by now a buyer for the McCormick mill. Returning home, he had interesting tales for Stephen about the sights of the Deep South. He described the oak trees with their

135

beards of Spanish moss, and the magnolia trees with wax-like blossoms, and the crêpe myrtles making a lawn pink with their dropping petals. He told about the plantations, where Negro slaves worked in the cotton and the rice fields, about lopsided cabins with chimneys from which smoke curled lazily. He described the sugar cane and the ribbon grass.

He told about New Orleans, the old Spanish and French city, describing the French market, where Creole ladies followed by Negro slaves came to select fresh vegetables and shrimps and crabs, bananas and coffee for their kitchens. He told about Congo Square, where at night black men speaking French worshiped the snake god of Voodoo.

When Mit was in town he and Stephen went often to the theater. Many traveling companies of players besides the minstrels came to Pittsburgh.

The famous actor Junius Brutus Booth brought Shakespeare's plays to the city of coal and iron, and the people cheered him and called him back for bow after bow. Mr. Booth was a very remarkable actor. He was not very tall, but he had something imposing about him, something which awed an audience. When he played the part of the hunchbacked Gloucester in *King Richard III* he spoke his lines with so much venom and malice and hate that the audience chilled and knew him for a monster. As Hamlet, he was sad, forlorn, perhaps a trifle mad. In the rôle of the unhappy Prince of Denmark he spoke lines

136

that Stephen Foster might well have pondered over:

> . . . to suffer
> The slings and arrows of outrageous fortune;
> Or to take arms against a sea of troubles,
> And by opposing, end them. . . .?

Poor Stephen never learned to end his troubles by opposing them. He was to pay a heavy price in later years for his indecision.

Mit and Stephen went also to see the actor Edwin Forrest. Forrest, besides being a great actor, was a man of common sense and uncommon insight. He sensed the desirability of more realism on the stage; to get it he had plays written especially for him. Many of these plays were on American subjects, with characters which, in contrast to those in most of the trite dramas of the day, were true to life. One of Forrest's made-to-order dramas depicted Andrew Jackson and the Battle of New Orleans. Mit and Stephen found a special interest in that play; for it was a matter of some pride to them that their father had with his own money outfitted a ship which took part in the celebrated battle for the Creole city.

Actresses Mary Ann Duff and Mrs. Alexander Drake came with theatrical troupes to Pittsburgh. They played in melodramas with queer names such as *Evadne,* and *The Somnambulist,* and *Adlegitha, or The Fruits of a Single Error.*

The two brothers went also to hear Henry Russell, the

famous singer of ballads. One of his songs made a deep
impression on Stephen:

> Woodman, spare that tree!
> Touch not a single bough!
> In youth it sheltered me,
> And I'll protect it now.

Most of Russell's ballads were very sentimental, the
kind of songs that the people of America loved in those
days. Foster, who, like most artists, was much influenced
by the popular taste of his day, wrote a number of such
songs. Only a few of them are remembered and sung
now. Like all very sentimental poetry, their lyrics were
built around false or shallow emotions, and their melodies had none of the deep feeling of his songs of home
or the simple sincerity of his Negro ballads. Foster's
genius, however, sometimes lifted a sentimental subject
out of the ordinary, as in the beautiful *Ah, May the Red
Rose Live Alway.*

Stephen attended regularly the meetings of the Knights
of the S.T. What "S.T." stood for, the members would
not reveal. Susan Pentland teased them by guessing that
they called themselves "Knights of the Square Table" in
imitation of Arthur's "Knights of the Round Table."
Whatever the secrets of their ritual, it was well known
that the boys met together primarily to sing. The songs
most popular with them were the minstrel ditties. Stephen
was particularly in demand. He had a pleasant baritone
voice, and he played the melodeon beautifully.

138

Friends

They sang such songs as *Zip Coon, Long-Tailed Blue, Coal-Black Rose,* and *Jump, Jim Crow.* They sang these songs over and over until they were tired of them. They wanted something new.

"I wish we could write songs!" wailed Andy.

For one whole week Stephen worked in his room at some mysterious task. He told no one except Mit what he was doing. When the night of the club meeting came around, he carried a roll of paper under his arm to the house where the members gathered.

Robert McDowell was making the old complaint. "There is absolutely nothing to sing that we haven't worn to tatters."

Mit could keep the secret no longer. "Yes, there is," he retorted. "Right here!" He took from Stephen the roll of paper and displayed it proudly. "My brother Stephen has written a song for us!"

The room was instantly noisy with cries of "Let me see it! Here, let's try it out. You take the tenor part, Andy."

Stephen, his cheeks flushed with excitement, played the introduction. The boys began to sing. They felt their way into the melody. As they felt surer of tune and words, their voices began to rollick along. The song was the happy-go-lucky *Lou'siana Belle,* Stephen's first minstrel-type composition:

139

He Heard America Sing

LOU'SIANA BELLE

Lou - si - an - a's de same old state, Whar

Mas - sa us'd to dwell; He had a lub - ly

cul - lud gal 'Twas the Lou'-si-a - na belle.

Chorus

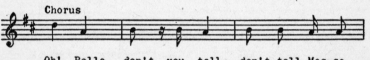

Oh! Belle, don't you tell, don't tell Mas-sa,

don't you, Belle, Oh! Belle, de Lou'-si - a - na Belle,

I's gwine to mar-ry you, Lou'-si - a - na Belle.

Second Verse
I went to de ball de udder night,
I cut a mighty swell;
I danc'd de Polka pigeon wing
Wid de Lou'siana Belle.

140

Friends

Third Verse	Fourth Verse
Dere's Dandy Jim ob Caroline—	Dere's first de B and den de E
I know him by de swell,	And den de double LL;
Tryin' to come it mighty fine,	Anodder E to de end ob dat,
Wid de Lou'siana Belle.	Spells Lou'siana Belle.

At the end of the song the young men crowded round Stephen with words of praise and wonder.

"Why didn't you tell us you could write songs like that?" they demanded. "That was jolly—as good as Christy's or Emmett's or Rice's songs any old day!"

Stephen was quietly happy, but he felt that his friends praised him too much, putting him beside the greatest minstrel song-writers of the day. It was a long time before Stephen learned the value of his own work, and several publishers were to make themselves well-to-do selling his songs before he thought to ask them for money for his little melodies. He believed his songs were good; it did not occur to him that they were great.

After *Lou'siana Belle,* melodies crowded into Stephen's mind more and more. The time of dreaming was over. By the time he was twenty, his days were filled with feverish activity.

One evening he appeared at the club with a composition which he had been working on for some time. It was a sad song, with a plaintive melody that brought tears to the eyes. This ballad, about an old Negro whose name was Uncle Ned, was one of the greatest songs Stephen Foster ever wrote.

He Heard America Sing

OLD UNCLE NED

Dere was an old nig – ga, dey call'd him Un– cle Ned, He's dead long a–go, long a– go; He had no wool on de top ob de head, De place wha de wool ought to grow.

Den lay down de shubble and de ho – o – oe And hang up de fid-dle and de bow. No more hard work for poor old Ned, He's

And hang up de fid-dle and de bow. No more hard work for poor old Ned, He's

142

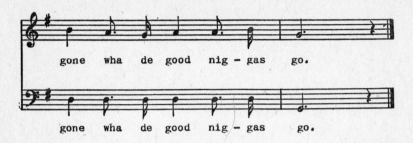

gone wha de good nig - gas go.

gone wha de good nig - gas go.

Second Verse

His fingers were long like de cane in de brake
  He had no eyes for to see;
He had no teef to eat de hoe cake,
  So he had to leave dat hoe cake be.

Third Verse

On a cold frosty morning poor Uncle Ned died,
  Master's tears down his cheeks ran like rain;
Caſe he knew when poor Ned was under de ground,
  He'd neber see his like again.

A few years later, when *Old Uncle Ned* was being sung all over America, *Dwight's Journal of Music* (issue of July 24, 1852) quoted a writer in the *Albany State Register*. This critic had written:

There is something in the . . . melodious "Uncle Ned" that goes directly to the heart, and makes Italian trills seem tame. . . . As for poor "Uncle Ned," so sadly denuded of his wool, God bless that fine old colored gentleman, who, we have been so often assured, has

"Gone where the good darkeys go."

143

CHAPTER TWELVE

GOOD-BYE

THE YEAR 1846 was drawing to its end. With the dry months past, the Ohio River had risen so that steamboats could at last descend the river without serious dangers from snags and sandbars. The wharves of Pittsburgh were lined with passenger packets and freight boats. Roustabouts were busy again, making the morning noisy as they rolled and carried the piled-up freight of the warehouses across gangplanks to the boiler decks of the steamers. The tall smokestacks of the boats shot up black smoke and sparks into the hazy November sky.

Crowds of men, women, and children had gathered at every landing to say good-bye to friends and relatives. They had brought gifts for the travelers—flowers and books and home-made cakes and candied fruits. Among the groups of women there was a good deal of quiet weeping into lace handkerchiefs, and among the men, considerable back-slapping and overloud laughter.

Strange to say, many of the travelers who were receiving such elaborate send-offs were going down river only fifty miles. Very few were going beyond Cincinnati or Louisville. Yet in many a mind was a fear that these travelers would never reach their destinations.

144

Good-bye

The steamboats themselves were the cause of the general uneasiness; for in that early day it was no uncommon occurrence for a boat to blow up. Boilers and pistons were sometimes imperfectly made; or they were abused by inexperienced or careless machinists and boiler men. Making hot steam to gain speed was a dangerous but frequent practice, and tying down the safety valve for the same purpose was not unknown.

Whatever the cause, a steamboat explosion was a hideous affair. The boilers were often blown up through all the decks, carrying with them the mangled and scalded bodies of passengers and crew. Those falling free into the river were sure to be drawn under the water by the eddying currents set in motion by the sinking boat, unless they were the strongest of swimmers or were fortunate enough to find some piece of freight to which they could cling.

Into the excitement and noise of the docks a carriage drove. It was a hired coach-and-four, with a big trunk strapped on the top. The black boy who drove the coach was proud that his fare was Mayor Foster of Allegheny with his family.

Stephen and Mit jumped out to help their mother down. She had grown thinner with the years, but there was amazing strength in her wiry body smothered in yards of old-fashioned dress goods. She wore a cashmere shawl about her shoulders, and a neat black bonnet on her graying hair.

145

Mr. Foster puffed and grunted as he climbed from the coach. He paid the coachman and superintended the untying of the ropes holding the trunk. Mr. Foster held firmly to the belief that if you wanted a thing done well, you did it yourself. When the trunk rested at last on the wharf, he called a porter to carry the hand baggage on board one of the steamboats.

Many friends had joined the boys and their mother. All the young men of the Knights of the S.T. were there; for it was Stephen who was going away. He was traveling to Cincinnati to become bookkeeper in his brother's warehouse there, Dunning being a partner in a firm of steamboat agents and commission merchants.

A barouche drove up, with a bevy of demure young girls who fluttered and gathered their skirts about them daintily and giggled in the way that young girls of that day thought proper and fashionable. The young men were quick to help them from the carriage. There was a great deal of commotion and a great deal of gallant talk that no one meant. Mrs. Foster smiled and enjoyed the frivolous speeches immensely. She would have called them refined and elegant—and probably did in her diary when she returned home.

Stephen was very quiet. Jane McDowell slipped over to his side. She was a beautiful girl, with a wealth of golden-brown hair, and grave brown eyes in a serious face.

"I wish you all kinds of luck, Steve," she said softly. "We shall miss you—more than you know."

Good-bye

Stephen smiled down at her. "Thank you, Jane. I shall miss you—and all the rest, too." He was not smiling any more. "I don't know why it is," he added, as if to himself, "but this place—my home—I am never happy away from it."

A puzzled expression came into Jane's eyes. She felt annoyed. It was like Steve, she thought, to save all his pretty speeches for his home. Another young man would have had a word for charming "Miss Jeanie" in her becoming blue bonnet.

A steamboat sounded its warning whistle. It was Stephen's boat. The group moved toward the gangplank. There Mrs. Foster cried as she told her youngest son good-bye, and Mr. Foster gave him some last-minute advice. Mit and the young men of the S.T. launched themselves into song. The girls joined them timidly for a line or two—then broke off, blushing as if they had done something very bold indeed. Stephen's fellow passengers turned smiling faces toward the group of serenaders, who were singing Stephen's own *Lou'siana Belle*.

Another whistle sounded and the gangplank was pulled in. The engines chugged faster and faster. The paddle wheel at the stern turned, beating the water into foam. Smoke poured black from the stacks. The young ladies on the wharf waved their handkerchiefs as the boat, with flags flying, got under way. Stephen stood at the rail until a bend in the river cut him off from the last view of home.

For a long time Stephen stayed on deck, watching the

147

soft colors of the river banks as the boat glided by. Trees grew right out to the water's edge, some with bare branches, others still wearing the yellows and browns and reds of autumn. The steamer passed little farms, with cabins set back among tall, symmetrical buckeye trees. Rickety landings and piers stretched out into the river. Smoke curled lazily from stone chimneys, and sometimes the odor of coffee drifted out to the boat from a kitchen where breakfast was being prepared.

The cabin passengers walked up and down the deck, talking about the weather, talking about politics, talking about business. Stephen stood apart and spoke to none of them. Now and again, one would cast a curious glance at the young man in his tall upstanding collar, well-fitted coat, and tight breeches—clothes in the latest fashion. He had taken off the tall hat to let the breeze play with his soft brown hair. Youth sat jauntily on his shoulders, but his eyes were sad.

Stephen stood at the rail until the boat passed the quaint village of Economy, where in 1824 a religious sect who called themselves the Harmonists had settled. They had built a church and many little homes. They still tilled the fields, which belonged to them all in common, and no one among them worked for wages paid by another. No man was rich and no man was poor in this little community.

When it was time for dinner, Stephen went to the dining-room through the "saloon"—as the large hall was called in which the passengers gathered. Fellow pas-

148

sengers greeted him with a smile or a grunt, according to their natures or the state of their digestions.

Stephen spoke very little. He was always shy and reserved when he was with strangers. While the others chatted, he studied the faces at the table.

There was a dark man with spotless linen frills along his shirt front and a diamond on his finger. His smooth, nimble hands bespoke the card-sharper and gambler. His destination was the Mississippi, where he would probably pick up a partner to help him "work" the big steamers bound for New Orleans.

Two of the middle-aged men were portly and prosperous-looking. They spent the dinner hour discussing Cincinnati's growing beef and pork distribution business.

There was a young married woman who had traveled all the way from New York. She had come to join her husband, who had gone before to buy a farm in Ohio. The captain and his wife took her under their wing, and asked her many questions about her trip across the mountains and about New York.

"La, la. What is the world coming to?" was the only comment the captain's wife could think of when the young woman told them about the railroad that crossed the Allegheny Mountains on the route from Philadelphia to Pittsburgh. In places its rails were laid on a narrow roadbed at the edge of a sheer precipice. Up its ten inclined planes, carriages were pulled, either by horses or by cables attached to huge drums turned by stationary engines.

149

When the young woman described the celebration held in New York for the opening of the Croton Water Aqueduct—which actually made it possible to pipe water through mains to hydrants at your very door—all the passengers fell silent to hear her. The New York aqueduct was the greatest feat of engineering up to that time, and everyone heard of "Croton water" with awe.

The young wife described the enthusiasm of the citizens of New York at the completion of the project. She told how the Astor House alone lighted one thousand candles as a salute to the engineers who had done what many had thought impossible. More than a million candles were lighted throughout the city. People danced and paraded in the streets. The volunteer fire departments demonstrated the amazing new water pressure. The celebration, like the aqueduct, was a huge success.

There were several young men no older than Stephen who were engaged in business in Cincinnati. Stephen listened to their earnest, knowing talk and wondered with a feeling of apprehension whether he would be a good bookkeeper.

Two other diners interested Stephen. One was a thin, sallow man with hair black and straight like an Indian's. The other was as round and talkative as his companion was angular and taciturn.

"The dark one," whispered the captain's wife to Stephen, "is an actor. His friend is a poet and song-writer."

The actor and the poet were talking at the moment quite seriously to one of the young men at their end of

150

the table. Bits of their conversation reached Stephen at the opposite end.

"Shakespeare, my dear sir, is being driven out of the theater by these abominable minstrel shows," said the actor, sourly. "We players of tragedy are hard put to it to make a living in competition with vagabond black-face comedians."

"And as for us," chimed in the plump one, "we who for years have been turning out chaste lyrics and ballads in no way offensive to the purest breast—" He paused to give the other diners time to appreciate his fine language. Clearing his throat, he continued, "We, I say, who have been supplying America with songs of delicate sentiment—we find our best efforts turned down by the public, whose debased taste seems to prefer trashy tunes like *Zip, Coon,* or *Root, Hog, or Die,* or *Old Uncle Ned.*" He suddenly pointed an accusing finger at the captain's wife, who looked uneasy and perplexed as to why he should single her out. "Would you believe," he demanded, "that just this morning I heard modest young girls so far forget themselves in a public place as to join in the singing of some vulgar minstrel ditty—something about *Lou'siana Belle?*"

Stephen's cheeks took on a deep red. Then his sense of humor came to his rescue. The thought of his songs, and the Knights of the S.T., and the laughing girls, all being condemned by the long-winded poet with the fat fingers brought a twinkle to his eye, and he suddenly decided to have his revenge.

151

"Perhaps," said Stephen, "you would favor us with one of your own compositions?"

The fat man looked enormously pleased. He did not require urging. He began to sing in a weak, trembling tenor:

"All, all alone I wander,
    Friendless and cold;
All, all alone I ponder,
    Lonely and old.
Does no heart beat with pity?
    Alas, I am forlorn!
Is no friend in this city?
    Would I had not been born!"

It was so funny to hear the well-fed man singing his doleful song that the diners smiled behind their hands or coughed into their handkerchiefs to keep from laughing. One by one they made excuses to leave. Stephen thanked the singer politely and made his escape as soon as he could.

On deck again, in the brisk air and warm sunshine, Stephen idly watched the river life. At one lonely landing a store boat was tied up. Calico-clad women with babies in their arms and older children tugging at their skirts crowded its deck; for it was a floating supply boat, where yard goods, pins, needles, yarn, boots, parasols, kerchiefs, and cheap perfumes could be bought.

Smaller boats tied up along the banks of the river to give the steamer right of way. The men and boys at the oars waved their caps in greeting. Negroes fished along the bank. Once Stephen caught sight of a little black boy riding along peacefully on the back of a patient old milk cow.

Negroes' songs floated across the river. At important landings the boat tied up and took on passengers, and then shoved off again with a parting salute from the steam whistle. More Negro songs followed them as they chugged down stream.

As the day passed, Stephen's homesickness left him. The quiet, lazy, friendly life of the river had brought him peace.

CHAPTER THIRTEEN

LA BELLE RIVIÈRE

THE CAPTAIN SPOKE to Stephen, whose brother Dunning he knew in a business way. "The pilot will welcome you up in the pilot house any time you care for his company," he said.

Stephen's eyes brightened. Talking with the pilot was a rare privilege. The pilot of a river boat was always a very interesting man, full of information about the river and the settlements along the banks. He was a sort of walking dictionary, encyclopedia, and history combined. As for the river, he read the turns, snags, sandbars, rapids, changing channels, and islands as if they had been taught him in school along with his A B C's.

Stephen mounted the stairs to the enclosed house between the stacks. The pilot's apprentice was at the wheel, while the pilot, Mr. Brown, lounged beside the stove. Without seeming to notice his "scrub's" handling of the boat, Mr. Brown was in reality on the alert for a single error. He greeted Stephen cordially, and pretty soon he was talking a blue streak to the young gentleman with the smiling eyes.

Mr. Brown was dressed neatly and in good taste, since his exalted position made him superior to all manual

154

labor. The pilot of a steamboat was the most important person aboard, and not even the captain dared to give him orders; for the safety of the boat, the cargo, and the passengers was in the hands of the shrewd man who could guide a boat through a dangerous channel even on the darkest night.

Stephen soon found that this particular man was stuffed with interesting information about the river, and that he could talk remarkably well. During this visit and several others following, Stephen learned much of the history of *la belle rivière,* as Mr. Brown always called the Ohio River.

"That is what the French explorers called the river," he explained. *"La belle rivière*—the beautiful river."

At Marietta, where the Muskingum joins the Ohio, the boat tied up to take on freight. Stephen, from his vantage point in the pilot house, watched the familiar activity at the dockside and listened to Mr. Brown's story of the town.

"Forty-eight men from Massachusetts started this town. They traveled overland in wagons along an old Indian trail until they came to the Youghiogheny River.

"In Pennsylvania they built boats on the banks of the Youghiogheny. They floated in these boats down the Ohio River to this spot. Here they landed and built a fortification of blockhouses and a double palisade. The Indians were supposed to be friendly at that time, but the settlers were taking no chances.

"They came in April, and by the Fourth of July they

were ready to celebrate the founding of a new town. There were great doings, and the savages from the forest edged up as close as they dared to look at the white men at their strange antics.

"First of all there was a procession of soldiers and citizens—just a handful of men in leather coats and buckskin leggings marching up and down in the wilderness and making as much noise as possible. No doubt the Indians thought them quite mad.

"After parading about they sat down to a banquet. The food was eaten in a bower of green saplings interlaced with vines. And that banquet on the bank of the Muskingum was a banquet that *was* a banquet! They had barbecued venison, buffalo steaks, bear meat, roasted pigs, and a pike six feet long. I got all this from one of those stout pioneers who helped eat it.

"The families of the forty-eight men arrived in August. And about this time the first sheriff of the Court of Common Pleas of the Territory took up his duties in the new town. That sheriff was Colonel Ebenezer Sproat. His job was to bring law and order to the Ohio, and he was big enough to do it. He was a giant of a man, at least six foot four inches tall. The Indians watching him were thoroughly impressed by his wonderful size. They called him 'Big Buckeye.' That's how it is that all natives of Ohio are called 'Buckeyes,' and Ohio the 'Buckeye State.' "

Leaving Marietta, the boat made its way on down the river. Stephen noticed here and there along the banks tall, rounded hillocks of earth that looked like giant mole hills.

"Lot of these mounds around here," explained Mr. Brown in answer to Stephen's question about them. "The Indians say they belonged to people who lived here before the buffalo grazed on the prairies. Can't say as I ever heard what they were used for."

The boat made its way along the deep channel of the river. The gentle hills of the valley rose sometimes as much as five hundred feet above the water. Along the banks, trees and shrubs, bare in the pale sunshine, waited for winter.

On the Kentucky shore Negro cabins squatted behind rail fences. Black mammies sat on rickety doorsteps, rocking babies in their arms. Little black boys and girls lined up to watch the steamboat go past.

The noise of the steamer disturbed long-legged birds that searched for slugs in the marshes along the shore. They rose with short, flapping wings above the reeds and mallows, uttering their strange, harsh cries. At the sound Stephen turned questioningly to his companion.

"Those are corncrakes," said Mr. Brown. "Feed on snails and grubs in the swamps and marshes. But they won't eat them if there's a corn field handy. And there's plenty of corn in Kentucky."

"Kentucky. What a strange sound the word has!" mused Stephen.

"It's an Indian word," explained the all-knowing Mr. Brown. "The Indians came from the North and East and

157

West to hunt game in this section, and when the tribes met there was sure to be war. They named it Kentucky, which some folks say means 'the dark and bloody ground'. Anyway, dark and bloody its pioneer history was—the pioneers fought for every square inch of that State."

After a while the channel narrowed and Mr. Brown had to take the wheel. Stephen went down to the saloon, where there was a piano. No one was about; so he sat down and ran his fingers lightly over the keys. *La belle rivière*—Ohio—Kentucky. The words stirred him deeply. Mr. Brown's tales of the towns along the bank of the historic river fired his imagination. He was glad that he was a part of that pioneering American people which had crossed the dark forests and had gone along unknown rivers with a song. A song. That was the important fact. Stephen was glad that wherever they went the American folk sang free, joyous music. He would write joyous music—music for men of courage conquering a wilderness!

Stephen began to play. When he came to the end of his song the saloon was filled with passengers full of curiosity. The happy, devil-may-care tune he had played they had never heard before; for Stephen had just made it up. It was *Oh! Susanna,* the song destined to be sung in a few short years in all parts of the world. Its second stanza immortalizes the *Telegraph,* a famous fast steamboat which in those days "trabbelled down de ribber"— down two rivers, the Ohio and the Mississippi.

158

La Belle Rivière

OH! SUSANNA

I came from Al - a - ba - ma wid my

ban - jo on my knee, I'm gwan to Lou - si -

a - na, My true love for to see. It

rain'd all night the day I left, The

weath -er it was dry, The sun so hot I

frose to death — Sus -an - na, don't you cry.

Chorus

Oh! Sus- an - na, Oh! don't you cry for

me, I've come from Al - a -

ba -ma wid my ban - jo on my knee.

He Heard America Sing

Second Verse

I jumped aboard de *Telegraph,*
And trabbelled down de ribber;
De Lectric fluid magnified
And killed five hundred nigger.
De bullgine bust, de horse run off,
I really thought I'd die;
I shut my eyes to hold my breath,
 Susanna, don't you cry.

Third Verse

I had a dream de odder night
When ebery ting was still;
I thought I saw Susanna,
A-coming down de hill.
The buckwheat cake was in her mouth,
The tear was in her eye,
Says I, I'm coming from de South,
 Susanna, don't you cry.

Fourth Verse

I soon will be in New Orleans,
And den I'll look all round,
And when I find Susanna,
I'll fall upon the ground.
But if I do not find her,
Dis darkie'll surely die,
And when I'm dead and buried,
 Susanna, don't you cry.

La Belle Rivière

Of course, Stephen did not write the words of this song all at one time. Later he added more verses, but the jolly tune came to him in a rush, as all his best music did.

When the passengers learned that the modest young man on board was a writer of songs, they gave him no peace. For hours he had to play and sing and he even ventured *Lou'siana Belle* and *Old Uncle Ned,* much to the discomfort of the fat man of the dinner-table conversation. The captain smiled as he looked at the merry crowd who leaned over the piano and joined in the choruses that the young musician taught them.

Stephen had to go back to the pilot house to escape the demands of the passengers. He was with Mr. Brown when the steamboat approached Cincinnati at nightfall of the second day. Torches flared along the Public Landing, looking like fireflies.

As the boat chugged slowly toward the distant lights, Mr. Brown told Stephen the story of the settling and naming of Cincinnati. "It was founded," he said, "by a group of twenty-six men just after the Revolution. They came down the Ohio River in barges and stopped at Sycamore Inlet, opposite the mouth of the Licking River. At that spot they made cabins out of the lumber of their barges. The site they chose was right on the trail over which the Indians had passed to and fro for centuries from the Great Lakes to the hunting grounds of Kentucky.

"The town they built was first named Losantiville. Someone with a smattering of Latin stuck together a lot

161

of 'roots'—as he called them—like bricks in mortar, and made a word which he said meant 'village opposite the mouth of the Licking'. New settlers pestered the living daylights out of the old ones, asking them what the name meant. So it was decided to rename the city.

" 'Cincinnati' was suggested by a group of officers who had served in the Revolutionary Army. They belonged to a society called 'The Order of the Cincinnati' in honor of the simple-mannered hero of the Roman Republic, Cincinnatus, who, though he preferred a quiet life on his farm to the duties of statesmanship, nevertheless left his plow when his country needed him. After the emergency was over he returned to his farm. Now George Washington, and other men of wealth and property who served in the Revolution, felt that they were something like Cincinnatus: they had left their estates to fight for their country, and after the war they went back to their farms. They had therefore banded themselves together as the Order of the Cincinnati.

"Well, it seems that the citizens of Losantiville were so taken by this idea that they let the Cincinnati have their way. It was certainly more convenient, because the new word was familiar to most people by that time, and the citizens didn't have to explain the name of their town to every Tom, Dick, and Harry that came down the river."

How the city had grown, thought Stephen, since he had seen it before! His first sight of it had been in 1833 when, with his mother and Henrietta, he had come through Cincinnati on the way to a visit in Augusta,

162

Kentucky. But he had been only a small child then, and hadn't really taken it in. Now his eyes were darting about the lively scene that the boat was approaching. For a full mile the lights of the flares extended along the wharves. Hundreds of steamers were tied up, waiting for the departure hour next morning. The noise of the roustabouts could be heard long before their shadowy figures under the pitch torches could be seen.

When the steamer docked, Stephen was the first to run across the gangplank. Throngs of people hurried round him as he stood with his baggage on the wharf. Suddenly two arms were about him in a bear hug.

"Steve! You rascal! Welcome to Cincinnati, the Queen City of the West!"

"Dunning! How are you? It's mighty good to see you. You don't look a bit changed, either!"

"What did you expect—an old man with a white beard? Come on. The Cassillys have driven down to meet you. You remember visiting them with Ma, don't you, years ago? And how is Ma? And Pa?"

And so, arm in arm, Dunning and Stephen walked along the wharf, happily talking of friends and home.

CHAPTER FOURTEEN

THE BOOKKEEPER OF CASSILLY'S ROW

FOR THE NEXT three years—that is, through 1849—Stephen followed the life of bookkeeper at No. 4 Cassilly's Row, where Dunning and his partner, Mr. Irwin, had their office and warehouse. Irwin and Foster were steamboat agents and commission merchants. Their store, like all the others on the Public Landing, was four stories high on the river side and three stories on the Front Street side. Stephen's stool and desk with ledgers were beside a window on the river side.

Cheerfully each morning he set to work, entering the articles of freight and the prices of shipment in neat letters and figures, and totaling the figures carefully. Sounds from the river pleased him. When he was not busy, he stuck his pencil behind one ear and walked to the window to watch the colorful life of the dock and wharf.

Hundreds of steamboats came and went. Whistles blew. Bells rang. Pilots in neat coats and snowy linen met in groups to talk over the details of their latest trip and to pass on helpful information about the river channel. Steamboat captains from gleaming hurricane decks superintended the loading of cargo. Black men toiled

164

under enormous boxes and crates, their faces glistening with the sweat of hard work.

Hotel omnibuses drove up, bringing porters who offered to carry the passengers' bags and trunks, while the drivers called out to advertise the hotels for which they worked. Little black boys were constantly underfoot, offering to sing or dance for a few pennies, or to take a message to any part of the city for a silver coin. Others had "poor man's sandwiches" to sell to the roustabouts at noon—great slabs of bread with beef or pork between. When the last crumb was gone, the Negroes lay back on the sacks and bales and joked with one another or sang songs.

Standing at his window one early spring evening, Stephen saw a young Negro and his sweetheart pass arm in arm along the Row. Their faces were so happy and their laughter so gay that Stephen smiled in sympathy. The image of those two sweethearts returned often to him, and later he wrote a whimsical little love-song—*Nelly Bly*—in memory of the dusky lovers of the river.

NELLY BLY

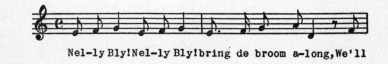

Nel-ly Bly! Nel-ly Bly! bring de broom a-long, We'll

sweep de kit-chen clean, my dear, and hab a lit-tle song.

165

Poke de wood, my la-dy lub, and make de fire burn, And

while I take de ban-jo down, Just gib de mush a turn.

Heigh! Nel-ly, Ho! Nel-ly, lis-ten lub to me, I'll

sing for you, play for you, a dul-cem mel-o-dy,

Heigh! Nel-ly, Ho! Nel-ly, lis-ten lub to me, I'll

sing for you, play for you, a dul-cem mel-o-dy.

Second Verse

Nelly Bly hab a voice like de turtle dove,
I hears it in de meadow and I hears it in de grove.
Nelly Bly hab a heart warm as cup ob tea,
And bigger dan de sweet potato down in Tennessee.

Third Verse

Nelly Bly shuts her eye when she goes to sleep.
When she wakens up again her eye-balls gin to peep.

166

De way she walks, she lifts her foot, and den she brings it
    down,
And when it lights der's music dah in dat part ob de town.

Fourth Verse

Nelly Bly! Nelly Bly! nebber, nebber sigh,
Nebber bring de tear drop to de corner ob your eye,
For de pie is made ob punkins and de mush is made ob corn,
And der's corn and punkins plenty lub a lyin' in de barn.

Stephen and Dunning boarded and roomed at the
home of Mrs. Jane Griffin. Not far away was the home
of the Cassilly family. The daughter of the house, Sophie
Cassilly, had a lovely soprano voice. An attractive crowd
of young people met at her home to sing and play the
piano. Stephen was soon a favorite with these young
men and women.

In the Cassilly drawing-room he composed and sang
his songs. He was always welcome to use the piano there.
In the evenings the young people gathered and made up
quartets and trios to sing Stephen's compositions. They
encouraged him with words of praise.

"Why don't you publish some of your songs?" said
Dunning one day.

"Who would buy them?" laughed the younger brother.

"Mr. Peters," suggested Dunning; "William C.
Peters."

Stephen considered the idea. He knew of Mr. Peters,
who had once taught music in the Foster home, but who

had left Pittsburgh in Stephen's babyhood. Since then he had set up a modest publishing business in Cincinnati, specializing in music.

"I could try," Stephen decided.

Feeling very nervous and self-conscious, he went to see his family's old friend, and offered two songs for publication: *Old Uncle Ned* and *Oh! Susanna.* There was no discussion of payment, for the songs didn't seem to Stephen to have much value—or, probably, to their publisher either.

After Mr. Peters had printed the two songs, he gave Stephen a few copies—and this was all the payment the composer ever received. But the sales began at once. The local newspapers praised the songs, and people started to buy them. Almost at once—to Mr. Peters' surprise—the first edition was sold out. He printed a second, and a third. Sales were greatly increased by the nation-wide popularity of *Oh! Susanna* during the California gold-rush of 1849; and within a short time Mr. Peters had made $10,000 from two songs that their composer had given him in exchange for a few free copies.

Stephen woke up one morning to find himself famous. It was a very pleasant feeling. Friends who met him on the street stopped to tell him how much they liked his songs. Strangers made excuses to meet him. People who did not recognize him passed by whistling or humming his music. Bright hope surged up in his heart. Life became suddenly very sweet. It is a good thing to be young and talented and appreciated, all at the same time.

168

Stephen had no regrets about not asking for money for his first songs. Fame was enough for the time being.

No matter where he was during those days, melodies popped into his head. Most of them were gay and youthful and full of happy laughter, just as Stephen was.

One day as he strolled along the wharf, he saw some Negroes dancing. One of them had such large feet that Stephen had to laugh at the sight. That was the beginning of a song. The song was *Oh! Lemuel!*

OH! LEMUEL!

Oh! Lem - u - el my lark, Oh

Lem - u - el my beau, I's guine to gib a

ball to - night, I'd hab you for to know; But

if you want to dance, Just dance out-side de

door; Be - cayse your feet so ber-ry large Dey'l

169

cov - er all de floor. Oh! Lem! Lem! Lem!

Lem - u - el I say! Go down to de

cot - ton field. And bring de boys a - way.

Chorus

Go down to de cot - ton field!

Go down, I say! Go down and call de

Nig-ga boys all: We'll work no more to - day.

Second Verse

Oh! Lemuel my hope,
Oh! Lemuel my joy,
I'll tell you who'll be at de ball,
My woolly-headed boy.
Dere's Nelly Bly, you know,
And Juliana Snow,
Dere's cane-brake Kitty likes de boys,
And she'll be sure to go.

The Bookkeeper of Cassilly's Row

Third Verse

Oh! Lemuel is tall,
Oh! Lemuel is fair,
Oh Lemuel has gone today
To take de morning air.
He makes de fiddle hum,
He makes de banjo tum,
He rattle on de old jaw bone
And beats upon de drum.

Homesick deck hands from New Orleans always sang of their longing for the South. Stephen caught the spirit of the life they longed for, and he translated it into melody in *Away Down Souf:*

AWAY DOWN SOUF

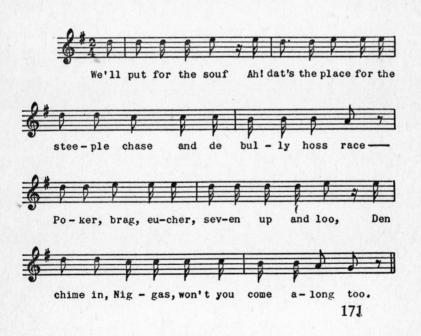

We'll put for the souf   Ah! dat's the place for the

stee-ple chase   and de   bul-ly hoss race——

Po-ker, brag, eu-cher, sev-en   up   and loo,   Den

chime in, Nig-gas, won't you   come   a-long too.

171

He Heard America Sing

Ideas tumbled over one another. The days of dreaming in Pittsburgh and Allegheny were bearing fruit. Before long Stephen began to realize that his songs were worth money. He signed a contract with Firth, Pond & Co., a publishing firm in New York City. By the time of his short visit to his Allegheny home, in 1849, he was a famous man, his pocket jingling with money that his music had earned for him.

Between 1846 and 1849, many changes came in the Foster family and in the world about them. In January 1847, Henrietta, whose first husband had died five years before, married Jesse Thornton of Youngstown. In that same month, Henry married Mary Burgess in Pittsburgh. In April, 1847, Brother William was appointed one of the three chief engineers of the Pennsylvania Railroad; their task was to begin the construction of trackage across the Allegheny Mountains. In June 1847, Dunning enlisted in the war between the United States and Mexico, and returned a year later ill with the tuberculosis that eventually caused his death. Mit during a visit to Stephen in the summer of 1848 fell ill of the dreaded cholera, and Stephen nursed him back to health. In 1848 gold was discovered in California, and by 1849 the great rush westward had begun.

None of these events affected the steady outpouring of Stephen's genius. The bookkeeper of Cassilly's Row faithfully added the figures in his ledgers, and in his spare time he wrote the most charming Negro ballads the world had ever known.

173

CHAPTER FIFTEEN

"ALL MERRY, ALL HAPPY AND BRIGHT"

STEPHEN MADE SEVERAL visits to his home in Allegheny during the years when he worked in the Cincinnati office. The boys and girls who had played and sung together had become men and women—some of them married and settled in homes of their own.

In January, 1849, Stephen attended the wedding of Isaac Pennock and Lizzy Grant. The next summer Andrew Robinson and Susan Pentland were married, and Ann Robinson and J. Cust Blair. Lovely Jane McDowell, who was often a bridesmaid, would toss her proud head and say she did not care if Steve never looked her way. The truth was that in those days Stephen thought only of music.

Between visits to Pittsburgh, he did his work conscientiously as bookkeeper for Irwin and Foster. While his brother was in the army he took full charge of Dunning's interest in the commission business. He went down to the docks and superintended the loading and unloading of cargo. He inserted advertisements in the local newspaper, telling of freight and passenger boats about to

174

sail. He solicited business. He kept neat books in his precise handwriting.

As soon as the work-day was done, he closed the office doors and set off with eager, swinging strides for his room. The evening was his own; then he was free to write songs that had come to him during the day, free to study and play the piano, the flute, and the violin. All of these instruments and others besides he played with skill and grace.

In the evenings there were parties and concerts. And there were minstrel shows.

The aimlessly wandering comedians of an earlier day had become the best-paid artists of the theater. The troupes were larger. Dan Emmett's "Big Four" had given way to Campbell's "Forty! Count 'Em! Forty!" The costumes were gorgeous. The stage settings were elaborate. The bands were deafening. And they advertised themselves without a blush as BIG! GIGANTEAN! SUPERB! MASTODON! FORTY! COUNT 'EM! FORTY!

Many an afternoon, as Stephen sat on his high clerk's stool beside the window overlooking the wharf, he heard the cry of the urchins on the dock: "Hey, fellers! Minstrels coming!" That meant that a steamboat with minstrels on board was nosing up to the Public Landing. As excited as any of the youngsters, Stephen would rush out bareheaded to see the parade.

On board the boat the minstrel band, forty strong, were playing at full blast. As the gangplank touched the

175

wharf, the minstrels filed across it to the tune of *Zip Coon* or *Yankee Doodle*. Each man wore a long-tailed Newmarket coat, of a gaudy pattern in yellow and black and with lapels of red silk, and a shiny "plug" hat. The drum major walked in front of the "silver cornet band." He wore a short red coat with gold braid and a towering shako of imitation bearskin. With a brass-knobbed baton he performed miracles of juggling and directing.

Two by two they marched through the streets of the city, to the hotel where they were to stay until time for the performance. Barefooted boys followed the parade. Businessmen came out of their shops to enjoy the bright, merry music. Everyone made plans to see the show which the huge banners advertised for 8:15 at the Opera House.

Stephen no longer went early to get a good seat at the show. He had become a privileged character; for he was a writer of minstrel songs. Most of the famous minstrels of the day—E. P. Christy, William Roark, "Daddy" Rice, and many others—were Stephen's personal friends. He was as welcome back-stage as any of the performers, and back-stage he could be found on any night when the minstrels were in town.

Long before the curtain was to rise, the stage was humming with activity. In the basement of the Opera House the band would be tuning up or rehearsing some new song number—possibly one of Stephen's latest. In the dressing-rooms the minstrels were blacking up. As they applied grease paint, which had largely taken the place of burnt cork, they joked with each other and re-

176

hashed the funny incidents of the last stand. Someone had missed a line. Someone had said the wrong thing. Some-one had forgotten about the change in the song. All these mistakes had been unpleasant at the time they occurred, but were funny in retrospect. How odd Bones had looked when Christy, on a bet, had given him the wrong cue! How cleverly he had covered up the mistake! *That* was showmanship! Stephen sat quietly and listened, feeling proud that these men, so quick to distrust the outsider, had accepted him as one of themselves.

Stephen often allowed his minstrel friends to sing his songs before they were published. Misunderstandings with publishers in regard to copyrights arose in later years because of Stephen's gifts, impulsively made, to his minstrel friends. The authorship of one of his finest songs—*Old Folks at Home*—was long in doubt because he sold to E. P. Christy the privilege of (Christy's) call-ing himself author and composer; though Stephen re-tained his rights in the song and took the income from its sale.

New performers were taking the limelight on the minstrel stages. Stephen heard Tom Christian, the first minstrel "yodeler." He saw the famous black dancer, Master Juba, who outdanced the blackfaced white min-strels by that perfect rhythm and timing instinctive in the African race.

Stephen listened attentively to the songs that each company brought. There were *Roaring Riber, Dandy Jim of Caroline, Stop Dat Knocking at My Do', Sailing on the*

Ole Canal, The Boatman's Dance, and hundreds of others. With these as his pattern, Stephen wrote many songs of his own. He gave his compositions freely to any of the minstrels who cared to sing them. There was none who refused, and it was not long before *Old Uncle Ned, Oh! Susanna, Lou'siana Belle,* and many others were as well known and as much at home in the gas-lit theaters as were the blackface artists who sang them.

For Stephen it was great fun knowing the performers and calling them by their first names. It was jolly to go with them after the show to some tavern where they ordered enormous and elaborate dinners in a grand manner and drank many a toast to the composer's health. It was fun to be called upon by these professional musicians to play the piano for them.

After the show, the happy-go-lucky wanderers sang for themselves and for Stephen, with their arms about his shoulders. His heart beat with happiness, and it was not until the early hours of the morning that he returned tired and blissful from these festive meetings with the men of the theater.

Tradition has it that during the years at Cincinnati Stephen made a trip which was to prove very important to his later song-writing: he went visiting one time at Bardstown, journeying, so the story goes, down the Ohio River to Louisville, where his cousin John Rowan, Jr., met him with the family carriage to take him to Federal Hill, the pleasant country estate of the Rowan family.

Stephen liked John Rowan. He was a handsome man

with a capable and charming way about him. Like his father, genial old Judge Rowan, John had chosen to take an active part in the government of his State, Kentucky, and of his country. A few years later he was made American Ambassador to the Two Sicilies.

As they drove along the pleasant country roads, Stephen recalled some words his father had spoken years before:

"I should like to have you visit Federal Hill, Steve. You are so fond of Negro music, and there you would hear as much of it as you wished; for Federal Hill is like a southern plantation, and there are many slaves belonging to the old Kentucky home of our kinsmen."

Stephen's eldest sister, Charlotte, had visited the Rowans shortly before her death. This same John Rowan driving his dappled grays along the dusty road had wanted to marry her those many years ago.

When they came in sight of Federal Hill, Stephen cried out in surprised delight.

"You like it?" asked John Rowan, his own eyes lighting with pleasure.

"Like it! I think I have never seen anything so beautiful." Stephen gazed with wondering eyes at the mellow old home.

"It was built in Revolutionary times," explained John Rowan. "It has been our home ever since. My father is buried on the grounds, under the crêpe myrtles he loved."

Graceful winding walks and a curving driveway approached the spacious old house on the hill. The sun was

179

setting, and its fire was reflected by the many-paned windows. There were shutters flanking the windows, and tall chimneys rising above the gabled roof. Vines made a lacelike tracery over the walls, and a wide flight of steps rose from the lawn to the welcoming entrance door. Tall tulip trees and maples lined the drive. Banana-shrub and crêpe myrtle perfumed the summer air.

An old Negro manservant took Stephen's baggage at the door, and in the spacious drawing-room John Rowan's wife and children welcomed their cousin.

"This is our family's man of genius," said John Rowan.

"Nonsense!" laughed Stephen. "I am only a writer of minstrel songs. Mother is even a little ashamed to have me sing them at home. I believe she considers my minstrel companions quite disreputable!"

Mrs. Rowan laughed her dissent, and—noting Stephen's instant interest in the house and its furnishings—turned the talk to these until dinner was announced. Then she led the way into the dining-room, with its high ceiling, heavy oak table, and tapestry-covered chairs. Here they were served bowls of rice with gravy, spoon bread, chicken, and early corn by two Negro girls with bandanas on their heads.

After dinner, John Rowan offered to show his guest over the estate. "We have a small plantation here," he said. "I doubt if you are familiar with a place that keeps slaves, are you?"

"No," said Stephen. "The Negroes I have known have all been free."

180

"Spoken like a Northerner," his cousin chided him. *"Free!"* He snorted and looked somewhat displeased; for, like many another southern slave-owner, he did not relish even the idea of Negroes who were not slaves.

Beyond the groves behind the house were the "quarters," as the double row of cabins for the Negro slaves was called on all plantations. Work was over for the day, and the Rowan Negroes were at home. Some of them were preparing their suppers. Stephen looked through open doorways and saw black mammies stirring pots in open fireplaces. Little black children rolled and played on the cabin floors. On the doorsteps of the cabins men and boys strummed their banjos in the warm evening air. All the slaves called "Ev'nin', Marse John" as he passed with Stephen.

The guest was shown the orchards and the gardens, the corn fields and the tobacco fields. There were hot-houses where Rowan experimented with new plants. There were tool-houses and blacksmith shops, and sheds for storing the produce. There were cows and horses, and barns with the sweet smell of hay. In the kennels were hunting dogs.

When they returned to the house, they found that some neighbors who had driven over for a chat with the Rowans were clamoring to meet the distinguished young Mr. Foster. Insisting that he play and sing, they gathered round him as he took his seat at the piano. For many hours he played for the Rowans and their friends, and for the Negroes who gathered on the porch and under the windows to listen to the simple, unforgettable melodies.

From his room that night Stephen looked out on a landscape of shadows and moonlight. Night birds called, and a light breeze rustled the leaves of the vines outside his window. From the quarters came the sound of singing voices. The music was soft, like a lullaby to comfort a fretful black baby. The composer climbed into the wide four-poster bed and let the voices of John Rowan's slaves lull him to sleep.

The memory of the peaceful plantation life at Federal Hill always remained with Stephen. United with other memories, it was in the course of time converted in the laboratory of the composer's mind and soul into that song of deepest feeling, *My Old Kentucky Home:*

MY OLD KENTUCKY HOME

"All Merry, All Happy and Bright"

bloom While the birds make mu-sic all the day. The

young folks roll on the lit-tle ca-bin floor. All

mer-ry, all hap-py and bright: By'n by Hard

Times come a-knock-ing at the door, Then my Old Ken-

Chorus

tuck-y Home, good night! Weep no more, my

la-dy, Oh! weep no more to-day! We will

sing one song for the old Ken-tuck-y Home,

For the old Ken-tuck-y Home, far a-way.

He Heard America Sing

Second Verse

They hunt no more for the possum and the coon
  On the meadow, the hill and the shore,
They sing no more by the glimmer of the moon,
  On the bench by the old cabin door.
The day goes by like a shadow o'er the heart,
  With sorrow where all was delight:
The time has come when the darkies have to part,
  Then my old Kentucky Home, good-night!

Back in Cincinnati, Stephen plunged once more into the writing of songs. He went to Negro churches to listen to the singing. He followed Negro funerals. He listened to the songs on the levees. Through listening, he came to understand the soul of a simple people pouring out their feelings in song. He learned how they played, and how they spent their hard-earned dollars. Having learned these things, he poured out his own feelings about them in beautiful melodies, with lyrics in Negro dialect.

Negroes liked horse-racing. So did everyone else in the South. Stephen wondered how it felt to be a Negro deck hand or roustabout with a week's wages in his pocket and a horse-race handy. He decided that such a man would be in high good humor, and the world would seem a friendly place. He would make jokes with everyone, and no one would care whether or not the joke were very good. Everyone would laugh, because everyone would feel the same way. What kind of song would a man like that sing? Stephen knew. He wrote the song and called it *De Camptown Races*. The funny exaggerations and gay foolishness of the song have made it a favorite with every-one who knows how it feels to be in holiday mood.

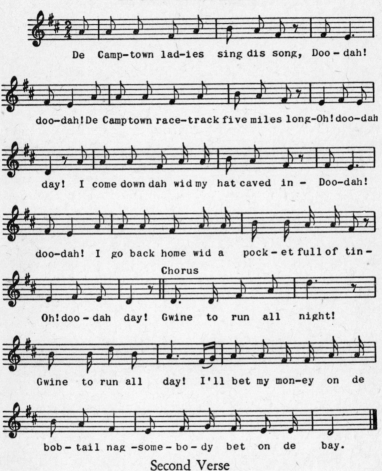

DE CAMPTOWN RACES

De Camp-town lad-ies sing dis song, Doo-dah!
doo-dah! De Camptown race-track five miles long-Oh! doo-dah
day! I come down dah wid my hat caved in - Doo-dah!
doo-dah! I go back home wid a pock-et full of tin-

Chorus

Oh! doo-dah day! Gwine to run all night!
Gwine to run all day! I'll bet my mon-ey on de
bob-tail nag -some-bo-dy bet on de bay.

Second Verse

De long tail filly and de big black hoss—Doo-dah! doo-dah!
Dey fly de track and dey both cut across—Oh! doo-dah-day!
De blind hoss sticken in a big mud hole—Doo-dah! doo-dah!
Can't touch bottom wid a ten foot pole—Oh! doo-dah-day!

185

He Heard America Sing

When the minstrels came to town again Stephen had two new songs to show them. They were Negro love songs. One was called *Nelly Was a Lady,* the other *Dolcy Jones.* The childlike simplicity and pathos of *Nelly Was a Lady* tugs at the heartstrings:

NELLY WAS A LADY

Down on de Mis-sis-sip-pi float-ing, Long time I trab-ble on de way, All night de cotton wood a-tot-ing, Sing for my true lub all de day.

Chorus

Nel-ly was a la-dy - Last night she died, Toll de bell for lub-ly Nell, My dark Vir-gin-ny bride.

Second Verse

Now I'm unhappy and I'm weeping,
Can't tote de cottonwood no more:
Last night, while Nelly was a-sleeping,
Death came a knockin' at de door.

186

"All Merry, All Happy and Bright"

Nelly Was a Lady and *Dolcy Jones* were published by Firth, Pond & Company. In December 1849, Stephen signed his first contract with these publishers. He felt at last that he could make a living by his music.

So there came a day when he said a final good-bye to his account books. On a cold January morning in 1850 he stood waiting on the Public Landing for a steamboat to take him to his home in Pittsburgh. Waiting, he watched other boats chug away from the landing.

A boatload of men bound for the gold fields of California set off down the river. They were going as far as Cairo on the Ohio, and then up the Mississippi to St. Louis. Thence they would travel on the muddy Missouri as far as Independence, and from there set out overland for the "diggings." Stephen watched the hardy men whose eyes were bright with the gold fever. As their boat pulled out they struck up a song. Deep, rough, untrained voices blended in robust harmony.

Stephen's heart beat faster. They were singing his song *Oh! Susanna*. But no—*was* it his song? It was the same tune, but the words were different. Ignorant of the composer's name or his very existence, these men, in the hearing of Stephen Foster, were making his little song into a real folk-tune.

Without knowing it, Stephen had written the marching song of the Forty-niners and the other covered-wagon pioneers. America sang her way to the Pacific with *Oh! Susanna*.

CHAPTER SIXTEEN

"*I DREAM OF JEANIE——*"

STEPHEN SETTLED BACK into the life of Allegheny and Pittsburgh with deep content. He was happy because his beloved family were around him. In the house on the East Common were his mother and father, with three sons—Mit, Stephen, and Henry, who was no longer working in Washington but had come home with his wife.

Stephen's song-writing had at last been accepted by the family as an undeniable fact. Worries about Stephen's future seemed to be over: he was making a living at last. The family adjusted itself in a slightly bewildered way to the fame of its youngest son.

As for Stephen, he was in high spirits. He went about with other young men on serenading parties, carrying a portable melodeon with him to set up under the window of the chosen house. Then he would play and his companions would join him in singing until they were invited to come inside and have cake and wine. There was much laughter and joking at these parties, and much praise for

188

Stephen. He wrote and sold two more Negro songs: *Angelina Baker* and *Way Down in Ca-i-ro*.

It was some time in the early spring that Stephen discovered Jane McDowell. Young men sometimes have a strange way with them. They see a pretty girl every day for months—at church, at concerts, at dancing parties. Then all of a sudden they discover she exists. They go about telling every one and wonder why no one else saw her before. It was so with Stephen.

The people of Pittsburgh smiled to themselves. They had watched Jane grow up, just as they had watched Stephen. They knew all along that she was a young beauty, with red-brown hair and golden eyes. They knew she was witty and "full of the Old Nick," as they said. They had admired her soprano voice when she sang in the choir and considered her very neat in her youthful ruffles and coquettish bonnets. They really thought that Stephen was a tiresome-long time discovering this winsome, graceful Jane McDowell, affectionately known to half the town as "Jeanie."

Stephen fell in love with Jane. He could not see enough of her. Every evening found him at the door of her home. Every evening the old Negro houseman at the McDowells' met Stephen with a smile of welcome. Taking Stephen's hat and the prim nosegay of flowers for "Miss Jinny," he shuffled down the hall to call softly at Jane's bedroom door: "Young ge'man heah to see you, Miss Jinny!"

189

The old Negro's name was Joe. He had grown old in service in the McDowell household. His kinky wool was white, and his eyes were tired and old. He stooped a little and he limped a little, and sometimes he had rheumatism. But he was never cross or complaining. He always had a smile for Miss Jinny and her beaux. But Stephen had a special place in his heart, and he showed his friendship in the warmth of his welcome when the young man came calling.

Joe had many a word of advice for Stephen. "Miss Jinny got plenty o' sperit. Any young man that win her heart got to speak his piece smart and peart. Don' take no for an answer, Marse Steve!"

The composer laughed and thanked Joe for his hint. "Some day," he said, "I'm going to put you into a song, Joe."

"Go 'long with you, Marse Steve! You-all be wastin' yo' time puttin' this old colo'd man in a song. Better improve yo' time an' write a song 'bout Miss Jinny."

As it happened, Stephen wrote both songs—one for Jane and another for Joe; not immediately, but later when he looked back upon the happy days of his courtship. And they are perhaps the most touching of all his compositions.

The old servant who carried the bouquets to "Miss Jinny" he made immortal in *Old Black Joe*. Faithful old Joe was dead when Foster composed his great song. The gentle voices had called him to the "better land."

190

"I Dream of Jeanie—"

OLD BLACK JOE

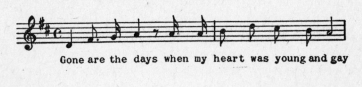

Gone are the days when my heart was young and gay

Gone are my friends from the cot-ton fields a —way,

Gone from the earth to a bet-ter land I know, I

hear their gen-tle voic-es call- ing "Old Black Joe."

Chorus

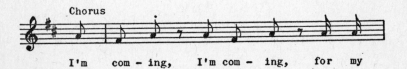

I'm com - ing, I'm com - ing, for my

head is bend - ing low: I

hear those gen-tle voi-ces call-ing, "Old Black Joe."

Second Verse

Why do I weep when my heart should feel no pain,
Why do I sigh that my friends come not again,
Grieving for forms now departed long ago?
I hear their gentle voices calling "Old Black Joe."

Third Verse

Where are the hearts once so happy and so free,
The children so dear that I held upon my knee?
Gone to the shore where my soul has longed to go.
I hear their gentle voices calling "Old Black Joe."

Stephen's courtship was swift and determined. Thus the story has been told, in later years, by a grand-daughter:

"At the same time Foster was courting her, she [Jane] had another attentive admirer, Mr. Richard Cowan. . . . One evening, owing to some miscalculation on Miss Jane's part, both called at Dr. McDowell's home at the same time. Steve came first. When Richard was ushered in by Old Black Joe, Steve promptly turned his back upon the pair, took up a book and read the evening through. . . .

"At ten-thirty calling hours were over in those good old days, and Richard, punctilious in all things, arose, wrapping his military broadcloth cape about him elegantly, he bid the forbidding back of Stephen a low, sweeping 'Good-evening, sir.' No answer from Stephen. Jane accompanied Richard to the door, feeling in her heart that a crisis of some kind was impending. She often laughingly said that when she came into the parlor that night, she scarcely knew where her sympathies lay, whether they had departed with Richard, or were present with Stephen. At any rate, she had small time for speculation— Steve had arisen, was standing by the table, pale and stern as she came in.

" 'And now, Miss Jane, I want your answer! Is it yes, or is it no?' And Grandma, nineteen in years, unused to quick decisions, made one then and never regretted it."

Stephen and Jane were married in July, 1850. At their wedding Jane's sister was bridesmaid and Mit grooms- man. It was a simple ceremony, and Agnes wrote of it to another sister, Marion:

"Jane is really married, and can it be possible? It seems so strange to me that she is married and gone, I cannot realize it still, and the wedding over. Jane and Stephen were pretty much frightened, Steve, quite pale. They each had to repeat some part of the ceremony after Mr. Lyman, which made it, I think, rather embarrassing.

"I was bridesmaid and Morrison, groomsman.

"We had a bride's cake which was very nice, two or three kinds of wine and ice cream. That was all, sufficient, too. All of Jane's dresses fit her beautifully and her other garments were made quite neatly. Sarah Kerr gave her a very pretty French work night cap. . . .

". . . I send you some bride's cake to dream on."

For their honeymoon, Stephen and Jane went to Baltimore and New York, traveling by stagecoach to Lewistown, and from Lewistown to Harrisburg by the Portage Railroad, where stationary engines or mules pulled carloads of people up inclined planes. Beyond Harrisburg they traveled on the Pennsylvania Railroad, for which Brother William was surveying a route to take the place of the old Portage across the mountains. Stephen and Jane were all eyes as they stared at the locomotive which was to pull their train. The little engine, with its tall stack sending clouds of smoke and hot sparks into the sky, was one of the first locomotives they had ever seen.

At Baltimore, Jane and Stephen visited places of historic interest in traditional wedding-trip style, not forgetting to pay their respects to the first railroad in the United States and the midget engine *Tom Thumb*.

Walking along the docks, they watched the little sailing vessels that made up Baltimore's famous oyster fleet. Riding at anchor, the boats looked like sea-gulls. The huge clipper ship putting out to sea with white sails billowing from the yard arms was a majestic albatross scooning along.

Before the couple left Baltimore they paid a visit to the grave of Edgar Allan Poe, who had died the year before in the city where he wrote his famous poem *The Raven*.

In New York, Stephen and Jane went to concerts at the famous "Castle Garden" theater. They rode in the cars of the first street railway in America. They visited Fraunces's Tavern, where George Washington took leave of his officers at the close of the Revolution. They watched with amusement the volunteer firemen of the Bowery strutting about with red vests, stovepipe hats, and long cigars, but Jane lifted her skirts and her nose in disgust when she was brushed by one of the great numbers of garbage-hunting pigs which acted as if they had been given the key to the city.

The two visited the shipyards along the East River, where more than ten thousand shipbuilders were at work on the clipper ships designed to take supplies around the Horn to the gold miners of San Francisco, or to make the long voyage to China for tea. The beautiful ships, with their long slender hulls, towering masts, and enormous sails, gleamed in the bright sunshine. With hundreds of other spectators, they watched the famous *Stag Hound* leave the harbor with her eight thousand yards of canvas spread to the breeze. The sailors manning her brought up her anchor with an old sea chantey:

> "As I was walking down Paradise Street,
>   Way-ay, blow the man down,
>   A brass-bound policeman I happened to meet.
>   Give us some time to blow the man down."

The sailors sang for the same reason that the river men of the Ohio and the Mississippi sang—to lighten their work. They had a leader who bellowed the verse. With the refrain, all voices joined him. "Way-ay—" All the

195

brown arms pulled together at the hawsers. "Way-ay—" Mighty shoulders heaved as the men thrust their weight against the capstan bars.

Jane and Stephen attended many concerts. They saw minstrel shows, too, and visited Stephen's publishers. Jane bought a new hat, and gifts of perfume and handkerchiefs for the friends at home. They went pleasure-boating on the Hudson River to watch the full moon making a silver path on the water.

When it came time to leave, they said good-bye to the exciting city with regret. By the eighth of September, the honeymooners were at home with the rest of the Foster family in Allegheny City.

For a time they were as happy as crickets. Stephen poured out his joy in two beautiful love songs. One was *Wilt Thou Be Gone, Love?*, a musical setting for the words of Shakespeare in *Romeo and Juliet:*

> "Wilt thou be gone? it is not yet near day.
> It was the nightingale, and not the lark
> That pierced the fearful hollow of thine ear;
> Nightly she sings on yon pomegranate tree;
> Believe me, love, it was the nightingale."

The second was a simple melody that might have been a little Irish tune:

"I Dream of Jeanie—"

SWEETLY SHE SLEEPS

Lento

Sweet- ly she sleeps, my Al - ice fair, Her

cheek on the pil-low pressed, Sweetly she sleeps, while her

Sax-on hair, Like sun-light streams o'er her breast.

Hush! let her sleep! I pray, sweet breeze, Breathe

low on the ma-ple bough! Hush! bright bird on her

win-dow-trees! For sweet-ly she sleep-eth now.

Sweet - ly she sleeps, my Al - ice fair, Her

cheek on the pil - low pressed.

Sweet - ly she sleeps, while her Sax - on hair, Like

sun - light, streams o'er her breast.

197

He Heard America Sing

Second Verse

Sweetly she sleeps, my Alice fair,
  Her cheek like the first May rose,
Sweetly she sleeps, and all her care
  Is forgotten in soft repose.
Hush! though the earliest beams of light
  Their wings in the blue sea dip,
Let her sleep, I pray, while her dreams are bright
  And a smile is about her lip.

Sweetly she sleeps, my Alice fair,
  Her cheek on the pillow pressed,
Sweetly she sleeps while her Saxon hair,
  Like sunlight, streams o'er her breast.

There were days when Stephen felt like shouting for pure joy. Remembering the gay, childlike Negroes who often felt the same way, he wrote a sparkling song called *Ring de Banjo:*

RING DE BANJO

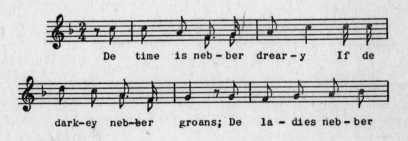

De time is neb-ber drear-y If de dark-ey neb-ber groans; De la - dies neb-ber

wea - ry wid de rat - tle ob de bones: Den

come a - gain Sus - an-na By de gas-light ob de

moon; We'll turn de old Pi -

a - no when de ban - jo's out ob tune.

Chorus

Ring, ring de ban - jo! I

like dat good old song, Come a - gain my

true lub, Oh! wha you been so long?

Second Verse

Once I was so lucky, my massa set me free,
I went to old Kentucky to see what I could see;
I could not go no farder, I turn to massa's door,
I lub him all de harder, I'll go away no more.

199

CHAPTER SEVENTEEN

THE DEEP SOUTH

IN THE FOLLOWING year—1851—a daughter was born to Stephen and Jane. They named her Marion. Jane bustled about the house from morning till night caring for her baby—bathing her, seeing to it that she was covered with soft blankets, singing to her. Stephen, watching, felt a little neglected. He began to feel worried, too. With a family of his own to support, he needed a steady income and a larger. He realized that he must work as he had never worked before.

Royalties from his songs seemed to melt away. As soon as they came they had to be spent for board and room, for clothes, for a nurse to look after little Marion. Determined to be businesslike, Stephen rented an office in Pittsburgh, where the baby's crying could not disturb him; then he bought a manuscript book and set earnestly to work to make a living.

The pages of that old manuscript book are witness to Stephen's careful workmanship. Some of the songs in the book take up six or eight pages and are a mass of crossed-out words and experimental notes. The composer expended as much effort over the lyrics of his songs as he did over their music. Like all true artists he knew that he

200

must work hard for sincerity and simplicity. The songs he wrote with simple, homely verses are the songs he rewrote most before they suited him.

Life was becoming more and more difficult. Jane wanted a home of her own. She was not happy with the family that Stephen loved. Stephen could not understand her discontent. He felt hurt. Jane went about looking unhappy. Thus matters dragged on for two years, while Stephen filled page after page of the manuscript book in which he set down almost all his compositions from 1851 to 1860.

It was Dunning who had imagination enough to understand the troubles of Jane and Stephen. This brother was no longer in the commission business, but was now a steamboat captain; and it occurred to him that a long steamboat trip would do the young couple good.

Stephen welcomed the idea, thinking, perhaps, that he and Jane might run away from the misunderstandings that had begun to make them both miserable. So it was that early in February of the year 1852 Jane and Stephen and a group of friends made a long trip down the Ohio and the Mississippi to faraway New Orleans on Dunning's own boat, the *James Millingar*. Among the holiday crowd were Susan and Andrew Robinson, Jessie Lightner—Mit's future wife—Mrs. William Robinson and her daughter Mary Ann, and Louisa Walker and her two brothers.

All the guests were musical. Gathered round Stephen at the piano in the "saloon," they sang the old songs and

201

the new. When they sang her husband's songs, Jane felt proud and forgot for a time that the praise of friends did not fill the cupboard at home. His wife's smile made Stephen glad. Resolutely he put behind him the nagging thought that though he was famous, he was still not making a great deal of money.

Down to Louisville they lazily floated. They stayed on deck while the boat went through the two-mile canal around the falls, and Dunning reminded them that not many years before boats had had to navigate the rapids— a dangerous bit of work even for a highly skilled helmsman.

When Dunning pointed out the infamous Cave-in-Rock, Stephen recalled and repeated to his friends the hair-raising tales that Mr. Foster had often related to his sons—tales of Murrell and other notorious robbers, murderers, and counterfeiters who had used the cave as a hide-out in an earlier day. Dunning added stories which he had picked up from river men and settlers along the banks of the Ohio. In the very early days of steamboating, pilots had dreaded to pass the eerie spot at night, when the candles and flares in the cave gave bold proof of the presence of murderers and thieves. Many an unlucky boat, grounded on a sandbar or caught by a wood island, had been dismantled by the pirates lurking at the cave, and no man of the crew left alive.

Dunning's guests shivered and were glad to get away from the dismal spot. Pleasanter scenes soon greeted

202

them. On down the Ohio they went. With singing and playing and dancing, they whiled away the hours.

At Cairo, where the Ohio joins the Mississippi, his friends surprised Stephen by singing his song *Way Down in Ca-i-ro*.

WAY DOWN IN CA-I-RO

Oh! la-dies don't you blush when I come out to play; I on-ly mean to please you all, and den I's gwine a-way.

Chorus

I hear my true-lub weep, I hear my true-lub sigh, 'Way down in Ca-i-ro dis nig-ga's gwine to die.

203

He Heard America Sing

Second Verse

Sometimes de nigga's life is sad,
  Sometimes his life is gay,
When de work don't come too hard
  He's singin' all de day.

Third Verse

Now we libs on de fat ob de land,
  Now we libs on de lean.
When we hab no cake to bake
  We sweep de kitchen clean.

Fourth Verse

Massa bought a bran new coat
  And hung it on de wall,
Dis nigga guine to take dat coat,
  And wear it to de ball.

Coming into the Mississippi, they entered a new kind of river life. They met and passed steamboats twice as large as the one on which they traveled. Instead of one paddle wheel at the stern the Mississippi steamers had two paddle wheels, one on each side. The paddle boxes covering the wheels bore the name of the boat in large letters. Massive and towering, with the blackest of black smoke pouring from their tall stacks, the Mississippi giants churned briskly up and down river. On their lower decks, Negro stevedores lolled on cotton bales, resting between docks.

Wider and wider grew the "Father of Waters." The banks were low, with luxuriant vegetation growing out to the water's edge. At night the shores were dotted with bonfires, and the dancing flames were reflected in a ruddy glow from the water.

As the boat came nearer to Natchez, Stephen stayed on deck most of the time, watching the life along the river banks—now he was seeing the Deep South for the first time. Federal Hill, home of the Rowans, had been but a pale copy of this colorful plantation life along the Mississippi. Yet, watching the armies of Negroes with plows and hoes in the fields close to the river, he had the feeling that he had seen them before. For this land of oak trees with trailing Spanish moss, this land of sugarcane and white-columned houses set in groves of magnolia and bay trees, this land of planters and slaves, had been made known to Stephen through the songs of the Negroes who worked on boats traveling to Cincinnati and Pittsburgh. The flavor of the South had already gone into his songs. Because he had the imagination of genius he had been able, without knowing actual southern scenes and manners, to write songs true to the experience of born-and-bred Southerners.

Pirogues flashed into the river from time to time—hollowed-out cypress logs, pointed at the stern and square at the bow, manned by skilled oarsmen from the bayous. Dunning told Stephen that these craft were the sole means of escape for the "swampers" when raging floods broke the levees and covered the surrounding country to the roof-tops with muddy Mississippi water.

Deeper into the South went the Ohio steamer, past Natchez, where the old Residence of the Spanish governor of Louisiana had boasted an outside circular stairway made of stones brought all the way from Spain as ballast in sailing ships. Beyond the swamps of the Yazoo River they made their leisurely way to Baton Rouge, named for the famous cypress tree that—so the story went—was so high that it could not be measured. French explorers had jokingly said it would make a good walking-stick; so as *Baton* (stick) *Rouge* (red, the color of its bark) the tree was thenceforth known to trappers and settlers.

The Fosters and their friends arrived in New Orleans in the Mardi Gras season, in time for the merrymaking on "Fat Tuesday"—so called because on that day the Creoles could eat heartily of everything and have a rousing good time before the self-denials of Lent.

Jane and Stephen and Dunning and the others rented costumes from one of the little shops near Royal Street. They dressed as Pierrette and Pierrot—as pirate captains with pistols—as ladies and gentlemen of the Court of Louis XIV—as Indian braves—as Spanish señoritas with tall combs and lace mantillas—as Chinese Mandarins: each according to his fancy and his purse. Like the other merrymakers in Canal Street, they put masks on their faces to give them the delightful freedom of anonymity. Very gay in their rented finery, they waited for the procession headed by Rex, King of Carnival, who sat high on a throne on a magnificent carriage pulled by six white horses.

Fairies and gnomes and witches and magicians and dwarfs and giants and every manner of fantastic personage followed the carnival monarch in carriages, decked with tinsel and flowers; and creatures hardly of this earth, with necks ten feet long and heads six feet high, walked in the street. Everyone was laughing and throwing confetti. A whole city had turned its back on work and care, to pretend that the world was light-hearted and young.

There was dancing in the streets, and everyone called gaily to everyone else. The balconies of old French houses wore festoons of flowers, and from behind grilled windows dark-haired Creole girls, like exotic flowers themselves, laughed down at the merrymakers.

That night Stephen and Jane and their friends went to the Rex ball, dancing until the light of early morning made the candles seem pale. Then with the other revelers they went to the French market to see the stalls opened for the day. Among the colorful displays of fruits and vegetables, flowers, cages of singing birds, herbs, baskets, crabs, and shrimp, they drank steaming cups of black coffee made over charcoal braziers. They bought pecan pralines from Negro mammies, and some baskets from Indians who sat woodenly beside their wares. Weary but happy, they made their way back to the boat with the sunrise.

While Dunning's boat took on cargo for the return trip, there was time for Stephen to see a little of the city near the bayous and plantations. Everything he saw he remembered, and his impressions went into some of his later songs.

In a hired hack he and Jane drove late one afternoon to the outskirts of town. Choosing at random an oak-bordered lane, they came, after an hour's drive, to a large plantation. "One little hut among the bushes," the "bees round the comb," the "dulcem melodies" of the slave hands returning home from the fields—all these things and more Stephen saw and heard as the hack horses clomped their way slowly past the "Quarters."

Early next morning Stephen was walking before breakfast beside the docks. He came upon an old Negro giving a group of roustabouts some advice. A broad-shouldered young Negro interrupted him to boast of his strength, and the old man rebuked him with, "It wuz swellin' dat bus' de poutin' pigeon." Observing that the same young Negro was neglecting his work, he added, "And it's a funny thing, but de jaw is de onliest part of de body dat likes to work!"

Stephen was sorry when the time came for the boat to return up the river. Standing on deck, he listened to the singing of the dock workers until the voices faded with the distance.

Before traveling out of the land of cotton and rice and cane, the steamboat docked one morning at a landing on which cotton bales were piled high. The roustabouts on the pier were strangely quiet as the boat nosed up, and did not sing out a greeting in their usual way. Instead,

208

they stood with serious faces turned toward a mournful procession passing along the riverside.

It was a Negro funeral. A pine coffin was carried along on the shoulders of eight stout men. Behind them, the mourners walked, two by two, in the same gingham dresses and overalls that they wore in the fields. Their heads were bowed, and they sang a dirge of deep pathos.

The music seemed familiar to Stephen. What was it? Suddenly he knew—here was part of a melody that he had heard in his childhood in Lieve's church. The rest of the dirge the mourners improvised as they walked sorrowing to the graveyard.

Stephen had used those same few bars of remembered Negro melody the year before. As the Negro mourners were doing, he had put them into a hymn for a funeral, calling the composition *Oh! Boys, Carry Me 'Long*. Of all Foster's music it is closest to the pathos and supplication of the Negro spiritual.

OH! BOYS, CARRY ME 'LONG

Oh! Car-ry me long, There's no more trouble for me. I'm bound to roam in a hap-py home Where all the dark - eys are free; I've

worked long in the fields, I've han - dled ma —ny a

hoe, I'll turn my eyes be - fore I die and

see the su - gar cane grow.

Chorus

Oh! boys, car - ry me 'long,

Car - ry me till I die,

Car - ry me down to the bu - ry - ing ground:

Mas - sa, don't you cry!

Second Verse

All ober de land
I've wandered many a day,
  To blow de horn
  And mind de corn
And keep de possum away.
No use for me now—
So darkeys bury me low:
  My horn is dry,
  And I must lie,
Wha de possum nebber can go.

210

The Deep South

Third Verse

Farewell to de boys
Wid hearts so happy and light,
  Dey sing a song
  De whole day long,
And dance de juba at night.
Farewell to de fields
Ob cotton, 'bacco, and all:
  I'se guine to hoe
  In a bressed row
Wha de corn grows mellow and tall.

One of Stephen Foster's very great songs was written in the manuscript book following his return from the Deep South. In Louisiana he had discovered a surprising feature of the slave system: when the master was kind, his slaves seemed to feel genuine affection for him and were apparently content with their lives of servitude.

Stephen had a vivid memory of the slaves at Federal Hill calling out greetings to John Rowan as he passed along the quarters. Remembering tales about genial old Judge Rowan, John's father, Stephen decided that he must have been one of the masters beloved of his slaves. Massa Rowan, lying buried under the crêpe myrtles— surely his darkeys had mourned his passing.

With his head full of such thoughts, Stephen wrote that poignant song of mourning, *Massa's in de Cold Ground*.

He Heard America Sing

MASSA'S IN DE COLD GROUND

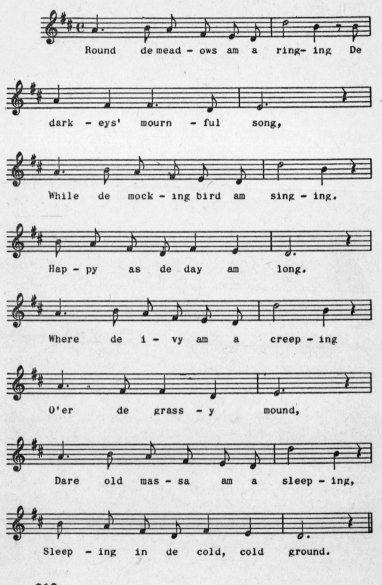

Round de mead — ows am a ring- ing De

dark — eys' mourn — ful song,

While de mock — ing bird am sing — ing.

Hap — py as de day am long.

Where de i — vy am a creep — ing

O'er de grass — y mound,

Dare old mas — sa am a sleep — ing,

Sleep — ing in de cold, cold ground.

The Deep South

Chorus
1st Voice

Down in de corn - field

2nd Voice

Hear dat mourn - ful sound:

All de dark - eys am a weep - ing —

Mas - sa's in de cold, cold ground.

CHAPTER EIGHTEEN

"BY 'N' BY HARD TIMES—"

STEPHEN AND JANE returned home to Allegheny to find the troubles from which they had run away waiting for them. They had now to face their difficulties.

Stephen wrote many songs in the months that followed. Though his music brought him a modest income, his expenses were often greater than his earnings. He had to borrow money—from Mit, from Jane's mother, from Brother William. He began the sad business of robbing Peter to pay Paul. These loans began to claim most of the money he received from the New York publishers.

Jane worried and fretted. Stephen became nervous and cross. When he worked, he demanded quiet. If Jane swept the floor while he was composing, he was annoyed. If a dog howled in the night, he could not sleep. At a concert, if one of the musicians played poorly, Stephen immediately rose and left the hall angrily, to the embarrassment of his wife and friends. He began to smoke constantly—so much that once his throat swelled almost shut and he nearly lost his life. He began also to drink a great deal.

214

Friends shook their heads over the change in the happy dreamer they had known. His family worried. They tried to jolly him into good humor, but it was not often that he broke from his moody thoughts to laugh with them.

Some of Stephen's suffering went into the writing of the famous song *Old Dog Tray*. This tender, melancholy song about a faithful old dog was inspired by a handsome setter which had been given the composer by a friend.

One day Stephen sat watching the dog playing with children on the East Common. The sad young man was thinking gloomily of his troubles. Because he could not be the gay companion of former days, many of his "boon companions" no longer welcomed him with the old warmth. His dog would not desert him merely because his thoughts had grown serious and his soul troubled.

> "Old Dog Tray's ever faithful,
> Grief cannot drive him away,
> He's gentle, he is kind;
> I'll never, never find
> A better friend than Old Dog Tray."

Stephen dashed to the piano. Feverishly he composed, his cheeks and his eyes burning with some inner fire. When he had done, he had written a great tribute in song to a faithful pet:

OLD DOG TRAY

The morn of life is past, And eve-ning comes at last; It brings me a dream of a once hap-py day, of mer-ry forms I've seen Up-on the vil-lage green, Sporting with my old dog Tray.

Chorus

Old Dog Tray's ev-er faith-ful Grief can-not drive him a-way, He's gen-tle, he is kind; I'll nev-er, nev-er find A bet-ter friend than Old Dog Tray.

216

"By 'n' by Hard Times—"

The composer's erratic moods grew upon him. There is a story that not long after he had written *Old Dog Tray,* Stephen was disturbed one night by the barking of a stray dog near the house. Furious because his rest was disturbed, he dashed out of the house in his night clothes and drove the animal away. Muttering angrily, the composer returned to the house to find Ma and Pa and Mit and Henry and Jane sitting in the kitchen, singing *Old Dog Tray.* It was their way of chiding him.

Stephen had to laugh. How funny and ridiculous he must have looked, he thought, running wildly after a poor old dog!

The years 1851 to 1856 were productive years for the composer. Some of his best songs were written during that period, and the sales of his published compositions mounted steadily. Stephen was recognized in America as a great man. His publishers welcomed his songs, and suggested that he move nearer their offices. So it was that Stephen and Jane and little Marion moved to New York.

All went well for a while, but the old homesicknesses that Stephen never in his life conquered came to him again. Mit has told us how it was:

After his marriage, Stephen received very flattering offers from the publishers in New York, and strong inducements to make that city his home. He removed there and had every favorable prospect that a young man could hope for. . . .

He went to house-keeping and liked New York very much. But after a year the old fondness for home and mother began to be too strong for him to overcome. One day he suddenly

217

proposed to his wife that they return to Pittsburgh. He brought a dealer to the house, sold out everything in the way of furniture, and within twenty-four hours was on the road to the home of his father in Allegheny. He arrived late at night and was not expected. When he rang the bell his mother was awakened and knew his footsteps on the porch. She arose immediately and went down herself to let him in. As she passed through the hall she called out, "Is that my dear son come back again?" Her voice so affected him that when she opened the door she found him sitting on the little porch-bench weeping like a child.

Stephen was at home again. For a few moments Jane was forgotten. Standing with little Marion in the shadows of the porch, she may have cried a little, too. No one knows. Perhaps Jane realized at last that love of home would always be the dominating emotion of Stephen's life—not his and Jane's home but that of his beloved parents. Bitter knowledge for the young wife.

One day Jane left the Allegheny household, taking little Marion with her to live with sister Agnes. Who knows what misunderstandings came between Jane and her husband? All that is certain is that one day she went away, with tears in her eyes. And Stephen, with tears in his eyes, stayed at home with Ma and Pa and Mit.

Etty sided with Stephen. She wrote a letter to Mit, saying: "How sorry I feel for dear Stephy, though when I read your letter, I was not at all surprised at the news it contained. I last winter felt that a separation was inevitable."

218

Dunning sympathized with Jane. He had once written Stephen that Jane was "a very sensible and interesting young lady." When he learned that they had quarreled and parted he spoke of "Stephen's foolish and unaccountable course."

Stephen, restless and at odds with himself, went back to New York. The publishers of his songs welcomed him. Firth, Pond, & Company agreed to take all the songs he wrote and to pay him more money.

Stephen worked hard, but the melodies that came to him in his lonely room in New York were not great. He wrote a sentimental song called *Little Ella* and a commonplace ballad called *Willie We Have Missed You*. He wrote a good deal of dance music—schottisches, jigs, and quadrilles. He prepared a collection of music for family use called *The Social Orchestra*. He created no beautiful melodies, however, and succeeded only in showing in his adaptations for *The Social Orchestra* his woeful lack of training in music.

During the lonely months in New York, Stephen went often to the theater. The conductor Louis Antoine Jullien was giving concerts at Castle Garden. Each night the orchestra presented an overture, a movement from a symphony, and selections from operas. Anna Zerr usually appeared as soloist, with a song or two.

Sitting with his eyes closed, Stephen would give himself up to the enjoyment of melody. One night he clapped loudly with the rest of the audience to call Anna Zerr back to the stage for an encore. The orchestra played a brief introduction. Stephen sat forward in his chair. Was it possible? Anna Zerr began to sing, and her song was his own *Old Folks at Home.* No one in the theater knew that the shy man who sat listening attentively with the rest was the composer of the beautiful melody.

"Way down upon de Swanee ribber—" sang Anna Zerr. Stephen was remembering how he happened to choose the name *Swanee.* His song had been written and was complete before he could settle on the name of the river. One day he burst into Mit's office to ask for a suggestion. It had to be a southern river, he explained, and the name had to be a word of two syllables. Mit took down an atlas from a shelf.

"What about *Pedee?*" he suggested. "That's a river in the Carolinas."

Stephen considered the name. It was hardly a poetic word. He shook his head.

Suddenly Mit's finger stopped in Florida. "What about *Swanee?*"

"That's it!" Stephen cried, and the song was done.

> "Oh! darkeys, how my heart grows weary,
> Far from de old folks at home—"

sang Anna Zerr.

Tears came to Stephen's eyes. Homesickness for Ma and Pa, the old folks at home, made his throat ache.

The audience applauded Anna Zerr. The critics writing in the newspapers the next day were not so kind. "We don't," said one of them, "like Mlle. Zerr's singing of 'Old Folks at Home.' True, she sings it only on an *encore,* but we think she sings it in bad taste; and we think, moreover, that it is bad taste for her to sing it at all."

There was an ill-natured comment in *Dwight's Journal of Music:*

We wish to say that such tunes (Old Folks at Home), although whistled and sung by everybody, are erroneously supposed to have taken a deep hold of the popular mind; that the charm is only skin deep; that they are hummed and whistled *without musical emotion,* whistled "for lack of thought"; that they persecute and haunt the morbidly sensitive nerves of deeply musical persons, so that they too hum and whistle them involuntarily, hating them even while they hum them; that such melodies become catching, idle habits, and are not popular in the sense of musically inspiring, but that such and such a melody *breaks out* every now and then, like a morbid irritation of the skin.

The critics were mistaken. The songs they attacked have lived on as beautiful and authentic expressions of deep emotion. They were mistaken; yet they had the power to hurt a great and sensitive spirit.

One critic, it is true, defended Foster: "I see," he wrote, "Miss Augusta Browne sneers at Negro melodies. Let her compose one which, like *Old Folks at Home,* shall be sung, played, and whistled from Maine to California,

221

in four months after it is published, and I will concede her the right to ridicule them if she likes."

One evening as Stephen sat alone he thought longingly of Jane. He remembered her as she had been in the days when Old Black Joe carried bouquets down the hall to "Miss Jinny." Thinking of her beautiful laughing eyes and her soft brown hair, he began to scribble words and music. For his wife he wrote *Jeanie With the Light Brown Hair*, a graceful little song of yearning and regret:

JEANIE WITH THE LIGHT BROWN HAIR

I dream of Jean-ie with the light brown hair, Borne, like a va-por, on the sum-mer air; I see her trip-ping where the bright streams play, Hap-py as the dai - sies that dance on her way. Ma-ny were the wild notes her mer-ry voice would pour,

"By 'n' by Hard Times—"

Ma-ny were the blithe birds that war-bled them o'er: Oh! I dream of Jea-nie with the light brown hair, Float-ing, like a va-por, on the soft sum-mer air.

Second Verse

I long for Jeanie with the day dawn smile,
Radiant in gladness, warm with winning guile;
I hear her melodies, like joys gone by,
Sighing 'round my heart o'er the fond hopes that die:
Sighing like the night wind and sobbing like the rain,
Wailing for the lost one that comes not again:
Oh! I long for Jeanie and my heart bows low,
Nevermore to find her where the bright waters flow.

Third Verse

I sigh for Jeanie, but her light form strayed
Far from the fond hearts 'round her native glade;
Her smiles have vanished and her sweet songs flown,
Flitting like the dreams that have cheered us and gone.
Now the nodding wild flow'rs may wither on the shore
While her gentle fingers will cull them no more:
Oh! I sigh for Jeanie with the light brown hair,
Floating, like a vapor, on the soft summer air.

CHAPTER NINETEEN

"... MY HEART GROWS WEARY..."

STEPHEN COMPOSED HIS love song for Jane some time in the spring of 1854. In October he was back in Allegheny. His heart was not so heavy as it had been, perhaps because he planned to persuade Jane to come back to him.

It was good to be at home again. Pa was ailing, to be sure, but he put a cheerful face on his troubles. Stephen noticed how much his mother had aged, and the fact saddened him. He was comforted when he saw that she seemed to be as active as ever, bustling about her household duties like a nesting wren. Mit was his dear old kindly self.

In the quiet of his study, inspiration once more dictated songs worthy of the composer's genius: *Hard Times Come Again No More, Come Where My Love Lies Dreaming, The Village Maiden.*

The real pathos of Stephen Foster's lack of musical training is embodied in *Come Where My Love Lies Dreaming,* a song rich and varied in melodic content. In the hands of a musician with a thorough knowledge of composition, it could have been expanded into a great piece of music.

With a new determination to be gay under all circum-

stances, Stephen wrote a devil-may-care song which, like
the early letter of his school days, revealed more of the
depths of unhappiness in his heart than he meant to show.
His friends, hearing the song, were deceived perhaps,
and thought that it was indication that the laughing,
dreaming, happy Stephen of former days had come back.
Mit alone may have suspected that his brother's song was
a kind of whistling in the dark to keep his courage up,
for into it Stephen wrote a spirit of bravado. He called
his song:

SOME FOLKS

Some folks like to sigh, Some folks do,
Some folks do; Some folks long to die, But
that's not me nor you. Long live the mer-ry
mer-ry heart That laughs by night and day, Like the
Queen of Mirth, No mat-ter what some folks say.

225

Second Verse

Some folks fear to smile,
　Some folks do, some folks do;
Others laugh through guile,—
　But that's not me nor you.

Third Verse

Some folks fret and scold,
　Some folks do, some folks do;
They'll soon be dead and cold,—
　But that's not me nor you.

Fourth Verse

Some folks get gray hairs,
　Some folks do, some folks do;
Brooding o'er their cares,—
　But that's not me nor you.

Fifth Verse

Some folks toil and save,
　Some folks do, some folks do;
To buy themselves a grave,—
　But that's not me nor you.

Stephen joined a Philharmonic Society. The young
men of the Society met often in taverns, where they sang
and ate and drank. They were a pleasure-loving crowd,
and Stephen was soon a great favorite. With these singing companions he began to waste much precious time.
He went often with serenading parties, singing a whole

evening away along the streets of Allegheny and Pittsburgh for the pure fun and companionship to be obtained. Not infrequently he drank more wine than his legs would support.

During that period of determined gaiety, tragedy came to the home on the East Common. Stephen's mother died suddenly in January 1855. Six months later her husband followed her in death. Stephen was broken-hearted. His world—the protected world of home, where he had always been surrounded with love and understanding—was swept away. The composer's youth was buried in the graves of his parents, and the puzzled, hunted look that grew more pronounced with the years came to his dark eyes.

Jane, seeing his suffering, was moved to pity. She patched up the old quarrel, and they went to housekeeping again, she and Stephen and Marion, renting Brother William's house in Allegheny.

The inevitable debts piled up again. Stephen wrote desperately, as the manuscript book shows, but money worries were gradually crushing his genius. In the years 1856 to 1859 he succeeded in writing only second-rate ballads. Not one of the great songs was written during that time.

During the trying days of 1856, Stephen wrote a song that gives us a glimpse of the sympathetic and kindly nature that made his friends love him in spite of his faults. The inspiration for this song was a tragic incident. The little daughter of a workman whom Stephen

227

called friend was running an errand on a stormy winter night. As protection against the driving snow she had wrapped her head in a shawl, covering even her eyes. Thus blinded, she ran under the feet of a team of horses pulling a dray, and was instantly killed.

Word of this reached Stephen just as he was leaving his house for an evening party. Without a moment's hesitation he gave up his plans and instead went to the home of the child's parents, there to stay through the long winter night and to give them what comfort he could. And later, in memory of this little girl, he wrote the plaintive song *Gentle Annie*.

GENTLE ANNIE

Thou wilt come no more, gen-tle An-nie,

Like a flower thy spirit did de-part; Thou art

gone, a-las! Like the man-y That have bloomed in

the sum-mer of my heart. Shall we ne-ver more be-

"... My Heart Grows Weary ..."

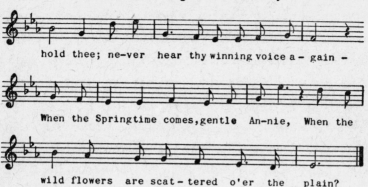

hold thee; ne-ver hear thy winning voice a-gain —

When the Springtime comes, gentle An-nie, When the

wild flowers are scat-tered o'er the plain?

Death came again to the Foster family. Dunning died in 1856. Henry, Stephen, and Mit went sadly together to Cincinnati to bring their brother back to Allegheny.

Terrible poverty came to Stephen and Jane and Marion. They were forced to give up the house on the East Common and move into a cheap boarding-house, where they lived, all three, for $7.50 a week. For the next few months their lives were a succession of moving days, from one dismal lodging-house to another.

The dreary, monotonous life of privation made Jane desperate. She determined to go to work. There was a young Scot in Pittsburgh who was superintendent of the Pittsburgh division of the Pennsylvania Railroad. His name was Andrew Carnegie, and he was to become one of the richest men in the world. But the year Jane screwed up her courage and applied to him for a job he was just a middling important executive. With a friend's help she had learned to send and receive the Morse code. Mr. Carnegie gave her a job at the Greensburg station a few miles from Pittsburgh.

229

Stephen's self-respect was hurt. In those days it was unusual for a married woman to work for her living. People condemned Stephen; he felt that many turned away to avoid speaking to him. It was a hopeless situation; for, though the sales of his songs mounted, his royalties were always too small to meet his needs. More and more often he went into the tavern to drown his sorrows in a cup of wine. For long hours he would sit alone, playing mournful music on his flute or violin. Only at infrequent intervals did the financial pressure let up. When it did, Stephen's kindly, fun-loving nature asserted itself, and he was gay and amusing once more.

Matters gradually went from bad to worse, however. Finally, Stephen said good-bye to Jane and Marion and went back to New York, determined to improve his financial condition.

History-making events were shaking the world. Abraham Lincoln had been elected President of the United States. The Confederacy was formed, and Jefferson Davis was elected as its President. Fort Sumter was fired upon. Lincoln issued a call for troops. The Civil War began.

Stephen was scarcely aware of the drama around him. He rode about the city streets of New York on the tops of horse-drawn omnibuses. With the wind blowing his soft hair, he sat thinking, thinking, thinking. Now and again as he rode thus a good melody came to him and he jotted it down in his notebook. A few of these songs were good, most of them poor. He published them all, and so it was he earned enough money to send for Jane and Marion.

For a year Stephen and his family boarded in various homes in New York—not lodging-houses, any more, but better-class establishments. The composer's large output of second-rate songs was making a living for the family. Once again life seemed brighter. Jane in later years told the story of those days in New York to her granddaughter, who wrote it down:

After moving to New York, they were at once drawn into musical circles. People entertained musically to a large extent in those days. There were balls, singing clubs, minstrels, and concerts, with invitations often to the Fosters. Wine flowed freely—like water. This is where Stephen C. Foster met the crushing defeat of his life. He was highly strung, temperamental, frail of physique. He sank rapidly where a physically stronger man might have survived. . . .

Although impatient and highly nervous as most people are who do creative work . . . on the day of a great New Year's Ball in New York, when my grandmother found her costume unfinished, he [Stephen] patiently sat all day and clumsily sewed spangles on her dress inwardly cursing (as Grandma could see) the needles which pricked his fingers. It was to be a Masque Ball. Grandma was dressed as a fairy Queen, but grandfather would not reveal to her his costume. All evening at the ball Grandma hunted him, but could not find him. Being young and a good dancer, she had no lack of partners, but her husband was missing. At midnight they unmasked,

231

when down from the stage came Foster; he had been playing first violin in the orchestra. With the aid of false whiskers and "plumpers" he had been entirely unrecognizable.

The period of comparative prosperity was brief. Stephen's income after a time became more uncertain, and finally inadequate. Jane once more returned to Pittsburgh to make her own living. Stephen, remembering the old gossip, remained in New York alone.

He rented a cheap room on the Bowery, that tawdry street where he could wear patched clothing and soiled linen and no one cared. Most of the money he earned he sent to Jane and Marion.

Sitting in a room for which he paid twenty-five cents a night, or in the back of a dingy grocery store, he wrote song after song. He set down pages and pages of notes, second-rate music for the most part, and line after line of mediocre verse.

Some of the songs he wrote were about the war. There were potboilers like *Our Willie Dear Is Dying.* The titles of some furnish a glimpse into Stephen's pathetic life at this time. One he called *Mine Is the Mourning Heart,* another *Farewell, Sweet Mother.* He was briefly hopeful with *Better Times Are Coming.* He tried to laugh again with the comic song *If You've Only Got a Moustache.*

Shortly before his death, he composed one song with the inspiration of his earlier genius. This beautiful love lyric with haunting music he called *Beautiful Dreamer:*

BEAUTIFUL DREAMER

Beau-ti-ful dream-er, wake un-to me,

Star-light and dew-drops are waiting for thee;

Sounds of the rude world heard in the day,

Lull'd by the moon-light have all pass'd a-way!

Beau-ti-ful dream-er, queen of my song,

List while I woo thee with soft mel-o-dy;

Gone are the cares of life's bus-y throng,

Beau-ti-ful dream-er, a-wake un-to me!

Beau-ti-ful dream-er, a-wake un-to me!

233

Second Verse

Beautiful dreamer, out on the sea,
Mermaids are chaunting the wild lorelie;
Over the streamlet vapors are borne,
Waiting to fade at the bright coming morn.
Beautiful dreamer, beam on my heart,
E'en as the morn on the streamlet and sea;
Then will all clouds of sorrow depart,
Beautiful dreamer, awake unto me!
Beautiful dreamer, awake unto me!

One of the few friends and companions of his last
years was George Cooper, who wrote the words for many
of the later songs. They lived from hand to mouth, writing a song in the morning, selling it in the evening for
enough money to buy a few meals. With a pathetic at-
tempt at brightening a gloomy situation with humor,
Foster called Cooper the "left wing of the song factory."

One raw winter day they set out in a snowstorm to find
a publisher for the song *Willie Has Gone to the War*.
Stephen had no overcoat. His shoes were old and cracked,
and the slushy snow soon soaked through the thin leather.
As he and Cooper passed Wood's Music Hall, the pro-
prietor hailed them from the lobby.

"What have you got there, Steve?" he asked, noticing
the rolled paper under his arm.

Stephen showed him the song. It was sold as he and
Cooper stood shivering in the wintry slush and cold for

234

ten dollars cash, fifteen dollars more to be paid at the box office that evening.

Stephen did not complain. Mechanically he wrote more songs. He cared nothing for food. Often he ate only an apple for his dinner. He lost interest in his appearance. Alcohol alone sustained him, after a fashion.

Because Stephen had not learned in his youth to struggle in the face of disappointment, he shrank from making the effort in those last years when his heart had grown weary. Because he was gentle and trusting and modest, he often did not receive the reward his genius deserved. Because he was lonely, he sought more and more to forget his melancholy life in drink. So it was that, as Edgar Allan Poe had done before him, he destroyed himself. His granddaughter wrote in years to come: "He suffered much and died for his fault."

Mit once came to see him. Shocked at Stephen's shabby appearance, the patched coat and cheap glazed cap, he said: "Steve, why do you go around looking so careless and unkempt? If I went around like that, I should be afraid of being insulted."

Stephen answered, "Mitty, don't worry so about me. No gentleman will insult me, and no other can."

One day George Cooper found Stephen lying very ill in the dingy basement room that he had been allowed to occupy rent-free. Stephen had fallen and had cut himself badly on a broken water pitcher. He must have been ill for many days, lying alone and neglected.

Cooper made arrangements to take him to Bellevue

Hospital. There Stephen was placed in a charity ward, and there he died on January 13, 1864, in his thirty-eighth year.

Trains and boats and coaches could not bring Mit and Jane to him in time. Before they arrived death had come a-knocking at the door.

The lovable, kindly, gentle writer of songs left to America and the world a wealth of rich melody and graceful lyric poetry. As for worldly goods, he left only a shabby purse containing thirty-eight cents—a penny for every year of his brief life. There was also a scrap of paper on which he had written, "Dear friends and gentle hearts." With those affectionate words, Stephen Foster, dear friend to all and gentle heart of song, bade his family, his friends, and the world good-bye.

Ring, ring de banjo —

Way down upon de Swanee ribber

Far, far away —

gone are the days